THE ROYAL HORTICULTURAL SOCIETY

CHELSEA

THE GREATEST
FLOWER SHOW ON EARTH

THE ROYAL HORTICULTURAL SOCIETY

CHELSEA

THE GREATEST FLOWER SHOW ON EARTH

LESLIE GEDDES-BROWN

A DORLING KINDERSLEY BOOK

To my husband, Hew Stevenson. With love and thanks.

A DORLING KINDERSLEY BOOK
www.dk.com

PROJECT EDITOR Joanna Chisholm
DESIGN AND PAGE MAKE-UP Mason Linklater
PICTURE RESEARCHER Jo Walton
SENIOR MANAGING EDITOR Mary-Clare Jerram
SENIOR MANAGING ART EDITOR Lee Griffiths
DTP DESIGNER Louise Paddick
PRODUCTION MANAGER Julian Deeming

First published in Great Britain in 2000
by Dorling Kindersley Limited, The Penguin Group (UK), 80 Strand, London WC2R 0RL
This revised edition published 2004
PROJECT EDITOR Claire Tennant-Scull

A CIP catalogue for this book is available from the British Library.
ISBN 0 7513 6974 8

Reproduced by Colourscan, Singapore
Printed and bound by Star Standard, Singapore

2 4 6 8 10 9 7 5 3

Half title page "NEW ENGLAND COTTAGE GARDEN", *Fiona Lawrenson, 1996.*
Title page "OLD ABBEY GARDEN", *Isabel and Julian Bannerman, 1994.*

CONTENTS

CHARLES
DE MILLS
GALLICA
OF ANCIENT ORIGIN

PREFACE

THIS YEAR, 2004, THE RHS CELEBRATES its Bicentenary. For 200 years the Society has led the way in gardening in this country. Chelsea, and indeed the Society's other flower shows, are part of a long tradition of shows dating back to 1827.

The first time I visited the Chelsea Flower Show as a newly elected Council Member, I went into the Floral Marquee and was totally mesmerised by it: the quality of the plant material was simply wonderful. When I became President of the RHS in 2002, I started to investigate the possibility of offering a special prize for an exhibit in the Floral Pavilions. This award – the President's Award – was presented for the first time in 2003. The criteria used in judging include aspects of design, creativity of the display and how the plants relate to each other as well, of course, as the quality of the plant material.

From the very first Chelsea show in 1913, it has been a showcase for an extraordinary richness of talent, new ideas and imaginative use of materials. This is the place to see new and exciting plants, to get tips from experts and to wonder at the colours of the overseas exhibits. Chelsea is always a dynamic show, and its exhibits reflect and challenge the changing tastes of gardeners. Over the last few years we have noticed a trend in people becoming interested in smaller gardens and the design of small gardens and so we have increased the number of smaller show gardens because these are now more relevant to many visitors.

Although Chelsea may have changed in appearance, the traditional aspects of the show continue and this book brings together highlights covering the years since the first show was held in 1913. The fascinating photographs offer a glimpse of the changing social scene in this country through that period and they also show that although there are many new plants and fresh ideas in garden design, the basic interests of gardeners remain much the same today as they were nearly one hundred years ago.

◁ THE PRESIDENT'S AWARD
Peter Beales Roses won the President's Award in 2003. Peter Beales was the very first recipient of the new prize.

President of the Royal Horticultural Society

FOREWORD: CHELSEA 2004

ANYONE WHO HAS DECIDED to modernise a much-loved and venerable institution knows that the way ahead is not easy. When the Royal Horticultural Society announced that it was to bring in the new millennium at The Chelsea Flower Show with a new marquee, it was the equivalent of *The Times*, after a couple of centuries, taking the advertisements off the front page and replacing them with real news. The British are a conservative nation: the uproar in both cases was enormous. With hindsight, the fuss seems remarkably silly: the show is much better for the changes.

Indeed, the show in 2000 was spectacular. Both the sponsors and the garden designers were determined to celebrate the millennium with show gardens that looked to the future with charisma and confidence and the whole ground was filled with inspiration.

The old and beloved marquee, made out of woven canvas and held together with guy ropes, was not only the biggest in the world — and therefore without much practical use anywhere but at The Chelsea Flower Show — it was made using the technology of 18th century sailing ships. It was about as up-to-date as the Cutty Sark. To the organisers it seemed obvious that the arrival of the 21st century was the moment for a touch of marquee modernisation. Yet Stephen Bennett, the Shows Director, knew all about the difficulty of shifting public opinion in favour of change; as he had introduced the

much-hated charges for members and the marquee one-way system. "We know that we won't get everything right the first time, especially as the show is so set in its ways. There will be further adjustment as we refine things until we achieve the optimum formula. Everyone, the media, our RHS Council and committees, the exhibitors and the public are all excited and keen to know how it will go. They are all positive because they know that the show can't stagnate. I am sure that the changes will give the show a fresh feeling."

Actually, in suggesting that all those involved were positive, Bennett was being optimistic. People, especially those least involved, are seldom positive about major change and what was happening in 2000 was probably the biggest change to the show since it moved to its Chelsea site in 1913.

THE DEMISE OF THE GREAT MARQUEE

In old catalogues, you will find a plan of the entire showground on the inside front cover and a more detailed one of the Great Marquee itself on the inside back cover. These diagrams changed so little that one year was virtually indistinguishable from the next. Since the first show, the overall plan has centred alternately around one large marquee and two large marquees. The famous Great Marquee was in place from 1951 to 2000 and by the end of the 20th century, the area under canvas covered about 80 per cent of the whole show site. Around its flanks and almost

RHODODENDRON
BUREAVII
Award of Merit 1939
Exhibited by Lionel de
Rothschild.

pushed to one side were the show gardens, which spread from the main entrance at the Bull-Ring Gate down the entire right-hand side of the ground. Much of the area on either side of Main Avenue was also devoted to show gardens, in addition to a major restaurant tent, displays of plant containers, tents for junior displays, amateur flower-arranging and professional floristry. Spread along the north side of the ground and Western Avenue were exhibits of powered machinery, greenhouses, conservatories, garden buildings, tools and furniture.

Beyond Eastern Avenue was the cool, calm and breezy area of Ranelagh Gardens, where bands played traditional music, where tired visitors came for a breather, or a picnic and where there were restaurants for the public, for exhibitors and for sponsors. It was here that the Royal Hospital was, until the new format arrived, keen to exclude displays and stands. But all that is history. The catalyst was the new three-dimensional interloper which, unlike its canvas predecessor, is rigid with egg-box like pinnacles poking up all over the roof. The new "Structure" as it is called will be used as long as it survives and no one is quite sure how long that may be. Almost certainly, however, longer than the 10 to 14 year life of each canvas tent. It is also far more adaptable than the giant marquee, in that it is made of a versatile series of small "tents" which can be moved about. The new structure was divided into two Floral Pavilions, which left the main axis of the ground open. From 2004, the structure is undivided and is known as the Great Chelsea Pavilion.

Inside the Pavilion, the space is simpler to navigate and more generous, with wider gangways – a necessary feature for the crush of visitors who flock to the show every year. Even better news for the show was that, along with the change of marquee, the whole space of Ranelagh Gardens on the east of the site was brought into play and the show expanded into its generous parkland. "We are, however," assures Stephen Bennett, "being careful not to destroy all the tranquillity of the one area where you can relax and get away from the hubbub."

This change, predictably, caused more problems for the organisers in that many exhibitors had hoped that Ranelagh Gardens would become a sales area for plants. The RHS, sensibly in my hindsighted view, decided firmly against adding sales to the delights of the show because it felt that the balance would be altered. This would, in turn, damage many of the horticultural exhibitors, whose main object has always been to promote their nurseries, garden centres, tourist destinations or societies. Instead, the extra space was given to improving the show's catering along with introducing new sites for those businesses that are allowed to sell their products, such as garden furniture, tools, accessories and ornaments.

MECONOPSIS
X SHELDONII
Award of Merit
1937

ADDED ATTRACTIONS

In an effort to even out the crowds, "the distribution of exhibits was changed," says Bennett. "We moved appealing stands into the northern, eastern and western areas. The cluster of show gardens in the Triangle used to excerbate the crowding problem; it was the honeypot of the whole show and had become too congested." The northern end of the Floral Pavilions was also given the added attraction of two show gardens.

This manoeuvre, however, has been less successful. Although the show gardens are more dispersed, many visitors have still not caught on to the idea. The main areas of show gardens, around the Rock Bank and Main Avenue, are now so crowded that a higher gallery has been built, yet in 2003, visitors were queueing for an hour for the chance to see the most popular gardens. At the same time, those show gardens which are not in the main viewing area seem to get far less attention.

On the other hand, I believe nearly everyone, (from public to exhibitors,) now agrees that the new structure is much nicer to be in. It is lighter and airier, and although many dislike the brashness of the design and stark white of the high walls, I believe the overall comfort has the edge.

Head of Show Development, Bob Sweet, is charged with looking at the overall mix of exhibits at Chelsea, and foresaw that the public would have to be won around. "We have to think how the public will perceive changes in the future. Some visitors are avid plant collectors who come because Chelsea is a serious gardening show, while others are attracted purely for the experience and they want to be looked after for the day." Sweet also worried that, with the departure of the old canvas marquee, some of the atmosphere would be lost. "I think that the Great Marquee had a sense of excitement: visitors would enter it expectantly, as if they were unwrapping a Christmas present. The damp grass and canvas had a special smell."

"My worry was always that the Floral Pavilions were too cutting edge and it would take a while to get the same ethos. They are considerably lighter than the Old Marquee. On a cloudy day it is brighter inside than outdoors and that gives the show a different atmosphere from any other British flower show." The way the inside exhibits are arranged has also changed, because the new structure has rigid walls which are 20-feet tall. To reduce the effect of all that blank wall, exhibitors have been discreetly sited so that those with taller plants such as lupins and delphiniums have stands that are placed towards the edges.

RETAINING SOME OLD CUSTOMS

As ever traditional, however, the RHS has ensured that some elements remain unchanged. "We are keeping what we call the valuable old junk. This includes the staging, generally of old orange boxes, wooden crates – even wooden ammunition boxes –

IMPROVED CONDITIONS

Despite complaints about the stark white walls and unfriendly demeanour, by 2003 most show goers agreed that the new structure was cooler, more spacious and helpful to exhibitors and visitors alike.

which have been traditionally used." For years to come, they will continue to emerge each May from storage at the RHS Garden Hyde Hall in Essex to be made into stands.

As a further change, after 2000 some traditional Chelsea exhibitors moved to the increasingly successful Hampton Court Show which is on a bigger site and is more commercial. It's perfectly possible, as Hampton Court comes to rival Chelsea not only as a day out for the family but a magnet for serious gardeners, that other parts of Chelsea will make the move along the Thames. Meanwhile, Chelsea has also been vigorously encouraging smaller (and more cheaply created) show gardens which are intended to show-case young designers and inspire those with small gardens. New features also include small marquees devoted to flower arrangers and specialist plant societies.

NEW AMBITIONS

Now the RHS is enviously eyeing the River Thames, a further natural extension for a show so crowded that it is always a sell-out. "We have suggested having catering on the Thames," said Sweet, "but, so far, it has not proved practicable. Then there is the marvellous open space of the South Lawn of the Royal Hospital, which we would love to use as a sitting area, and we don't think would be a nuisance to the Chelsea Pensioners. But we do want to retain all Chelsea's charm and atmosphere and ensure that the annual excitement is not lost. We know our visitors don't like change, so we are determined not to lose that quaintness."

With the stands under the bright white new Great Chelsea Pavilion still composed of wartime ammunition boxes, that seems unlikely.

BRAVE BEGINNINGS

" *Whatever else we go without,*
we should not go without a
Chelsea Flower Show. "

GOLD MEDAL 1914
Notcutts gained this Gold at the
second Chelsea Flower Show.

THE CHELSEA FLOWER SHOW came about practically by accident, as have many great traditions. The world's most famous flower show might have been the Inner Temple or Holland Park Flower Show, or even the Wembley Flower Show had events worked out differently.

The first Royal Horticultural Society (RHS) Great Spring Flower Show at Chelsea opened in May 1913, although, confusingly, there was another May flower show – the Royal International Horticultural Exhibition – held at the Royal Hospital in 1912. This one-off event was backed but not run by the RHS, which cancelled its own Great Spring Show for that year.

The RHS Great Spring Flower Show had normally been based at the Inner Temple in the heart of London, and the RHS was still expecting to stage its 1913 show there, even though the Society

had a brief flirtation with the idea of moving to Holland Park. RHS Council minutes for 25 October 1910 show that Lady Ilchester had agreed a fee of £250 for the use of her Holland Park grounds and, by 19 December 1911, a deal seems to have been reached. However it came to nothing.

The RHS was distinctly unhappy with the idea of staying at the Inner Temple because – a common theme throughout its history – the show was becoming too big for its site. The lawyers were not keen to continue hosting the show, either: they seem to have resented the colour, the jollity, and the sight of people enjoying themselves in the Inner Temple grounds. As one bencher (Inner Temple lawyer) complained, dry law and moist plants were not natural allies. Neither did they appreciate the sweet papers, the wafts of hot soup, and "quasi-Oriental concoctions" brewing on

catering stands. Gradually the Inner Temple lawyers added ever more stifling restrictions to the RHS contract: no advertisements on the railings without their consent; all handbills had to be shown to the Inner Temple authorities for approval; and no unseemly food in the tea tent.

The break came soon after the RHS had agreed to cancel its own 1912 Great Spring Flower Show. The Rev. W. Wilks, RHS Secretary, wrote to the Inner Temple to say no show would be held that year but that the President and Council "hope that nothing may occur in the interval of 1912, on either side, to prevent the resumption" of the

ROYAL INTERNATIONAL HORTICULTURAL EXHIBITION

Mr Louther, Lady Cranbrook, and friend view this one-off show at the Royal Hospital, in May 1912.

show at the Inner Temple in 1913. The benchers responded with yet more conditions, and the RHS began seriously to look elsewhere – encouraged by the huge success of the Royal International Horticultural Exhibition's one-off event at Chelsea in 1912. By July 1912 the RHS President Sir Trevor Lawrence had met Major General Crutchley of the Royal Hospital at Chelsea, and the two began to talk about a 14-day reservation of the gardens and a 14-year agreement. At the RHS Council meeting the following month, 13 August 1912, all had been decided. The show would move to Chelsea for 1913. The Council then turned to more pressing matters: primulas and experiments in electrical cultivation, for which the RHS would be "put to no expense whatsoever".

Piggott Bros, the Society's tent contractors, were clearly horrified by the timetable. It would be impossible to put up the tents in 14 days; they needed 28. By October, 28 days had been agreed. Piggotts would be paid £690 for the tenting. Johnson, Kiddle & Co. would print 5,000 posters for £85 and 70,000 cards for a further £52, and Stokes would arrange the carting for £70. Iron sockets would be let into the ground to take the uprights of a large tent – Piggotts having acquired permission from Major General Crutchley. The Royal Artillery Band was to be engaged to play music throughout, and a circular was to be sent to sundriesmen.

Considering that the Chelsea Flower Show now takes at least 18 months to organize, the RHS was running a tight schedule if it was to be ready in time. At the end of April, a press luncheon was arranged for Monday, 19 May (a tradition that continues to this day). With only a fortnight to go until the show

ROSA 'PAUL'S SCARLET CLIMBER'

First Class Certificate 1915

Exhibited by William Paul & Son.

GOLDEN START

This impressive azalea garden in 1914 was the first of many displays to have won Gold Medals for Notcutts of Woodbridge.

opened, the committee agreed that bath chairs should be allowed in, from 9am to 12 noon on the second day, for five shillings extra.

THE FIRST SHOW OPENS

Despite the rushed planning, the first RHS Great Spring Flower Show at the Royal Hospital, Chelsea, successfully opened on Tuesday, 20 May 1913, for three days. Curiously there is no Council report on how this show actually went. The Minutes of 17 June indicate that the Royal Hospital complained that the grounds had not been "properly reinstated". It also noted that the Duke of Marlborough was to be given an unprecedented 500ft (150m) to show his orchids in the 1914 show, and the Royal Artillery Band was rehired for that year. Finally the Council recorded that some orchid pollen had been stolen and, as a

consequence, medals had been withdrawn from the guilty parties.

The *Gardeners' Chronicle*, which provided the best written records of the early shows, was more forthcoming. The first Chelsea "had exceeded all expectations". The tent, it reported, was 300ft (100m) long and 275ft (80m) wide, taking up six spans and over 2 acres (0.8 hectares). Of a total of 73,000sq ft (6,780sq m), more than 21,000sq ft (1,950sq m) were allotted to 84 large groups of flowers, plants, and shrubs, with another 7,500sq ft (696sq m) used for 95 exhibits on tables. There were 17 large rock, formal, or paved gardens arranged in the open air. In all there were 303 exhibits organized by 244 exhibitors, compared with a mere

PLANTS FOR SALE

Notcutts had owned their nursery in Woodbridge for 15 years by the time they issued this catalogue, in 1912/13, just before the first Chelsea Flower Show.

EARLY OFFICIALS

A group of RHS staff in front of the Enquiries tent at the first Chelsea, 1913. H.R. Hutchinson (the Librarian) is standing in the centre while S.T. Wright (the first Director of Wisley) is seated second from the left.

25,000sq ft (2,322sq m) and only 126 exhibitors at the Society's Inner Temple show in 1911. Everyone was very pleased. "We were again witnessing an international display of the world's horticulture," the *Gardeners' Chronicle* enthused. "Some of the rock gardens appeared as if formed to last a generation ... The Chelsea site should become as nearly perfect as is possible for mortal affairs to be."

Queen Alexandra, Princess Victoria, and the Duchess of Fife toured on the first day. Among the famous plants on display were *Rhododendron* 'Pink Pearl' on Waterer's stand, *Clematis* 'Nellie Moser' on Jackman's stand, and a display of lilacs, rhododendrons, and Japanese acers shown by Notcutts. A *Meconopsis delavayi* won a First Class Certificate for Professor Bayley Balfour, and Fletcher Bros were awarded the same for the *Cupressus lawsoniana* 'Fletcheri' (now known as *Chamaecyparis lawsoniana* 'Fletcheri'). Blackmore & Langdon who, like Notcutts, still

RHODODENDRON 'ALICE'

Gold Medal 1913

exhibit to this day, won a Gold Medal for their display of begonias, and Dobbies acquired one for their sweet peas. The Hon. Vicary Gibbs (a name that features widely in the early archives) received a Gold – or rather his gardener Edwin Beckett did – for a display of vegetables including 'Duke of Albany' peas, 'Golden Perfection' tomatoes, radishes, beet, marrows, and – years before the chef Elizabeth David was known – purple and long white aubergines.

At the end of May 1913, the *Gardeners' Chronicle* was able to add that the Chelsea Show had been the most successful in the Society's history, with a total income of £3,000 (the Temple show having produced a meagre total of £1,400 in 1911), with gate receipts of some £2,150.

By early 1914 the Chelsea tradition of intense media interest was becoming established. The Council agreed that there should be "cinematography" at the show if there was a favourable offer from a film company; Sir George Holford agreed to approach George V and Queen Mary to visit on 19 May; and, the Council heard on 5 May, the *Daily Graphic* was to print a special Chelsea issue. The charge for the toilets was set at two pence rather than one penny. Although King George and Queen Mary had by then said they could not visit – they had a date in Aldershot – Queen Alexandra, widow of Edward VII, announced that she would. A disgruntled exhibitor had not been given the site he was promised, so a rule was now made that no such pledges were to be given.

The 1914 show, reported the *Gardeners' Chronicle*, was even better than 1913: the weather was warm, and *Lilium regale* won an Award of Merit. The Hon. Vicary Gibbs won a Gold Medal with a vegetable display that included Chilean beet, globe artichokes, and kohlrabi.

Unfortunately war clouds were gathering. Archduke Ferdinand and his wife were assassinated at Sarajevo only a month after the show ended. (The couple had visited the 1912 Royal International Horticultural Exhibition at Chelsea – the Archduchess being a keen gardener.) In August 1914 the First World War was declared. The nephew of the RHS President, Field Marshall Lord Grenfell, was killed in action in September, and the RHS staff were asked to give money to help keep their enlisted staff on half pay. A German spray for gooseberry mildew was, meanwhile, blacklisted.

The 1915 show was a sad affair, with steady rain, mud underfoot, and waterfalls from the tent roof. The railway companies had been quite incapable of delivering the essential rocks and plants on time for the show, so exhibitors had found other ways to bring them to Chelsea. Lady Dundas, a charitable fund raiser for war victims, arranged for Viscount Dalrymple, then a small boy, to parade around the grounds on a Shetland pony to collect money for the war. The Hon. Vicary Gibbs won another Gold Medal with Edwin Beckett's golden waxpod beans, marrows, and broad beans, and the Hon. John Ward (whose gardener was Charles Beckett – were they related?) received a Silver-Gilt Medal for "melons splendidly netted, sloe-black grapes, and cardinal nectarines," wrote the *Gardeners' Chronicle* of 29 May 1915. The RHS, which in 1911 had refused to allow ladies to its banquets, now recognized that lady gardeners existed, and acknowledged the necessity to dig

for victory. In 1915 it even organized a show of women's work at the Horticultural Halls.

As the war deepened, the RHS struggled on. By November the Council had removed King Ferdinand of Bulgaria as an honorary fellow and, the following February, decided that tickets should remain at ten shillings for the first public-access day (and at two shillings and sixpence after 6pm), with two shillings and sixpence on the second day (and one shilling after 6pm), and one shilling on the third day of the show.

GREAT SURVIVORS

Blackmore & Langdon is one of three nurseries that have exhibited every year since the first Chelsea Flower Show. Here two of their workers, Walt Rivers and Bill Pocock, on arrival at the showground in the late 1930s, remove protective cotton wool from their famed begonias.

LADY DALRYMPLE

The charity organizer Lady Dalrymple talking with her friends at the 1914 show. In the next two shows her son was to ride round the grounds on a Shetland pony collecting money for victims of the First World War.

By March 1916 the RHS was wondering whether to cancel the whole event because of the cost of the new entertainment taxes, but Lord Balfour said it would benefit trade. At this time, the RHS was also given the sad task of working on the layout of war cemeteries in France. The 1916 show was therefore very downbeat: it had no great tent, alcoholic drinks were not allowed on the exhibitors' stands, and the theme was Hardy Flowers for Wartime. The band refused to play German music; instead they favoured Elgar and Gilbert and Sullivan. There was only one show garden; and the Hon. Vicary Gibbs turned from vegetables to scented-leaved pelargoniums. The weather, ironically, was glorious and brought out Queen Mary and her daughter Princess Mary on the Tuesday, and Queen

Alexandra and Princess Victoria the following day. Viscount Dalrymple – dressed as a colour sergeant of the Scots Guards – rode his Shetland pony once more to raise money for the war effort. Attendance on the opening day was twice that of 1915, and the show was "a notable demonstration of what may be accompanied in the face of very difficult circumstances". It made a small profit of £400 against the 1915 loss of £1,040. In 1917 the RHS abandoned the show, citing new entertainment taxes as a reason, and Chelsea was suspended for two years.

AFTER THE FIRST WORLD WAR

The First World War had been over for only six months when the 1919 Chelsea Flower Show opened, following a vote "overpoweringly in the affirmative" to start up again. The producer Léon Gaumont asked and gained permission to film the event. Queen Alexandra and the deposed Empress Marie of Russia arrived on the first day with the Duke of Connaught and teams of Belgian, French, and Dutch horticulturists, possibly impressed by the voluntary collections of money to buy seed for their devastated fields. The horticulturist Ellen Willmott, whose offers of show tents the Council seemed constantly to turn down, won a First Class Certificate for *Paeonia willmottiana* (now known as *P. obovata* var. *willmottiae*), raised from seed discovered in China. An Award of Merit was given to *Rosa* 'Paul's Lemon Pillar' just in time to celebrate George Paul's 58th year of showing roses at RHS meetings – this rose having been named by the Victorian rosarian William Paul. (The two Pauls do not appear to have been related.)

During 1919, the RHS was approached by General Kentish, who said that he needed the Chelsea land as a sports ground for 5,000 troops. Would the Society surrender the lease? Only if the Army offered enough money, came the reply, and left the site as good as it found it. No more was heard from the General, and the RHS remained at the Royal Hospital.

By 1920 another tradition – of inevitable complaints – was established: the RHS President Lord Lambourne told the annual press luncheon that "there were always those who grumbled no matter what the Society did". He presumably meant the press itself, who then as now were unhappy with the way the tickets were distributed, and the exhibitors, who constantly protested about the conditions including lack of display and storage space. Old ladies, the exhibitors moaned, were always occupying the seats reserved for their assistants.

Two tenting contractors were asked to submit quotes in 1920: Piggott Bros, who had provided the tents since the beginning, said £945, while Messrs Hawley underbid them at £675 and won the contract. The RHS also reviewed other more spacious sites for their May show, including Holland Park, for which Lady Ilchester refused to drop her fee below £550. They also considered Lambeth Palace for a July show but nothing came of that, either.

THE LONDON SEASON

Chelsea was an important part of the London Season from the first show. Here visitors admire an outside exhibit in May 1915.

By 1923 the RHS was again wondering about moving and discussed going to Wembley on 10 February, but by 17 February they had voted 45 to 15 against. The weather that May was "execrable" and the Chelsea site during the show was "a quagmire of thin, liquid mud – practically impassable by ladies", reported the *Gardeners' Chronicle*. This made the RHS ponder yet again the suitability of the site.

Meanwhile in 1921 Edwin Beckett had won a Gold Medal and a special Silver Lindley Medal for his plants. "In cultivating and exhibiting he has no superior," said the *Gardeners' Chronicle*. The following year, with the Hon. Vicary Gibbs, he received not only a Gold Medal but also Special Congratulations and the Cain Cup for the best amateur exhibit. In 1923 the pair showed seakale beet, globe artichokes, endive, and capsicum. "King George spent a considerable time at this exhibit and congratulated Mr Edwin Beckett on what [the King] described as 'a most wonderful exhibit'." Beckett was awarded yet another Gold. The next year he showed a 'King George' cucumber.

Beckett cooked and preserved his vegetables too and, when challenged by a show visitor in 1925 to prove that the vast size of his vegetables did not spoil their flavour, he responded by asking the lady to a meal of them. The vegetables passed the test. To cope with the increasing popularity of the Chelsea Flower Show, this 1925 one was held over a trial five days, rather than the traditional three.

The following year (1926) produced another problem: the General Strike. Fortunately it ended just in time for the Flower Show to go ahead, on 25 May – postponed by one week and reduced to three days. The *Gardeners' Chronicle* reported that it was larger than ever. Messrs Pulham & Sons won the *Daily Graphic* Cup for the best rock garden – an award that appears to have been offered only once.

As the experimental five-day opening in 1925 had proved unpopular with exhibitors, the show became a four-day event in 1927, when an extra day, especially for RHS members, was instituted. This was to be on a Tuesday, and the public were allowed in only from Wednesday to Friday. At that Chelsea the Hon. Vicary Gibbs and Edwin Beckett had switched from showing cut vegetables arranged in artful patterns; instead they displayed capsicums as pot plants and fruiting aubergines. The year after, the duo won the Sherwood Cup for the best exhibit, for vegetables such as 'Wonder of Italy' tomatoes, 'Di Vernon' and 'Climas' potatoes, and 'Jasper Queen' cucumbers. This was the coldest Chelsea on record, with hail, pelting rain, and thunder.

In 1929 Chelsea reflected garden styles that would be seen more than 50 years later: great set pieces in which hardware and design were as important as the planting itself. Mrs Sherman Hoyt, from Pasadena, tried to show the Californian deserts as they really were by importing three different gardens, for which she won a Gold Medal. She then donated her set pieces to Kew and gave $1,000 to the RHS. Edwin Beckett showed morel fungi and redcurrant tomatoes in this 1929 show.

He and the Hon. Vicary Gibbs built their final stand in 1930, Beckett warning everyone that it would be the last. No one believed him because he had said this so often, but the *Gardeners' Chronicle* did illustrate the stand, which was laden with rows of cauliflowers, leeks, turnips, marrows, beetroot, endive, lettuce, mustard and cress, mushrooms, and French beans. Yet again it won the Sherwood Cup for the best exhibit, and this time Beckett did retire. At the same show, Ellen Willmott (who, with Gertrude Jekyll, were the first women to be awarded the Victoria Medal of Honour) was

POCKET-SIZED GARDENS

An inter-war feature of the Chelsea Flower Show was miniature gardens displayed on raised stands. Here, umbrellas aloft, some visitors in 1939 consider the skills involved in such gardening.

Mrs Sherman Hoyt of Pasadena
pioneered today's show gardens
with her enthusiasm for
Californian deserts, which she
exhibited at Chelsea in 1929.

so impressed by the roses she was judging that she wished she could give each an award.

ECONOMIC TRENDS

Each Flower Show at Chelsea has tended to mirror the prevailing conditions: thus after the First World War one popular type of plant – the costly "stove plants", which grew only in heated greenhouses and needed considerable gardening skill – virtually vanished because labour was scarce. In the Depression in the early 1930s, edible plants such as herbs and vegetables were popular. In 1935, to celebrate George V's reign of 25 years, a Jubilee Trophy was awarded to the best exhibit by an amateur. Lionel de Rothschild won this, and his two gardeners, Francis Hanger (a future curator at Wisley, in the 1940s) and R. Finlay, were given £20 each. The New York Horticultural Society also offered a trophy for the best exhibit of trees and shrubs, which was won by Hillier Nurseries.

In 1937 the RHS chose an Empire theme for Chelsea, to celebrate the coronation of George VI and Queen Elizabeth. The *Gardeners' Chronicle* was dubious about this, suggesting it was a little dull for

the general public. It does not sound it: the displays, which were amassed by J. Coutts (the curator at the Royal Botanic Gardens at Kew) were from Australia, New Zealand, India, Canada, Newfoundland, the Seychelles, Africa, Palestine, and the West Indies. "It far exceeds the Royal International Horticultural Exhibition of 1912," reported the *Gardeners' Chronicle*. Although there were two more shows before war was declared in September 1939, the 1937 one was the last great show before the Chelsea Flower Show closed from 1940 to 1946.

After the Second World War, the RHS President Lord Aberconway told a gathering of former exhibitors in October 1946, "Whatever else we go without, we

REGAL TRIBUTE ▷

For the coronation of Queen Elizabeth II in 1953, the Women's Voluntary Services created a floral crown in the garden of a Pre-fab.

◁ IMPERIAL THEME

To celebrate the coronation of King George VI, exhibits from all over the British Empire were assembled for the 1937 Chelsea Flower Show.

should not go without a Chelsea Flower Show next year." The problems of organizing the show in only seven months were immense: gardeners had gone to war; glass was needed for blitzed buildings rather than greenhouses; and Britain was gripped with austerity and rationing. During the war Britain had been seriously bombed for the first time, so exhibits addressed the problems of what could be done with bomb sites around St Paul's Cathedral, in the City of London. Lady Seton (Julia Clements) recalled, "It was such a vast exhibit of colour and that was wonderful after the drabness of war. I was judging flower arrangements. That year Lord Aberconway introduced some of the things we had seen in the USA, such as flower-arrangement exhibits illuminated in niches of corrugated paper. But there was really no flair about the show. Nothing was

three-dimensional. All the exhibits were on one level of tabling in the Great Marquee, because the RHS had not yet realized the value of presentation."

Lord Aberconway with his gardener at Bodnant, F.C. Puddle, won a Gold Medal for his group of 40 hybrid rhododendrons. He was the second member of his family to achieve the Victoria Medal of Honour – the third being the late Lord Aberconway, RHS President 1961–1984 and, a past President Emeritus of the RHS.

Sid Cox, then a nurseryman with Hillier's, was exhibiting for the first time in 1947. "We needed nine lorries to take our exhibits to Chelsea." One of his favourite displays – of rhododendrons from Exbury, the gardens of Major Edward de Rothschild – was also much admired by George VI, a keen rhododendron man himself.

RAFT OF FLOWERS
*Water features have been common
to Chelsea from the first. Visitors
in 1958 admire a moored dinghy
filled with rhododendrons.*

ROSA PEACE
*('Madame A. Meilland')
First Class Certificate 1948
Exhibited by Messrs Wheatcroft.*

Members of the public who turned up for the show paid from two shillings and sixpence to ten shillings on Wednesday, 21 May 1947, and were serenaded by the Band of the Grenadier Guards, playing Tchaikovsky's *Valse des Fleurs* and Waldteufel's *Christmas Roses*. Interestingly these ticket prices were similar to those for the first day some 30 years earlier. Possibly after its seven-year closure, the RHS was keen to attract back its regular affluent clientele as well as a wider section of the general public, who might have small gardens of their own.

The following show (1948) was still very much scarred by war. The Women's Voluntary Services (WVS) created a cottage garden around a Pre-fab, with helianthus, salvia, and astilbes at the front, and vegetables at the back. Messrs Wheatcroft showed off the rose PEACE ('Madame A. Meilland').

In 1951 the RHS proudly announced that the Chelsea Flower Show would have the largest marquee in the world – covering 3.4 acres (1.4 hectares). For the Coronation of Queen Elizabeth II, in 1953, the Royal Botanic Gardens at Kew organized a special Commonwealth exhibit, with exotic greenery from far-flung countries as well as an English woodland glade. In 1954 the Duke of Windsor bought plants for his house in France; in 1955 the *Gardeners' Chronicle* reported, "not for 30 years has there been such a cold, perverse spring with night frosts". In 1959 the show received a touch of modernism from *The Times* "Garden of Tomorrow", "with the most modern aids to

LABOUR-SAVING ATTRACTIONS
Robot gardeners were put through their paces in The
Times *"Garden of Tomorrow" in 1959 (above) and
again in 1994 (right), on the Husqvarna stand. At
neither show did these machines attract the large orders
that their manufacturers were seeking.*

horticulture". These included a radio-controlled lawn
mower (you guided it from a deck chair), electric bird
scarers, watering devices, and frost protection.

In 1960 plants were three weeks ahead of their
normal season and the RHS President Sir David
Bowes-Lyon told the press that Chelsea "was bursting
at the seams with not nearly enough room for us".
Another tradition – aristocratic vegetable growing –
was also returning: Col. E.J.S. Ward's gardener, H.J.
Dodson of Hungerford, and another private estate
were showing "something we have not seen at
Chelsea for many years". At the 1964 show, Col.
Ward's stand contained 70 varieties of 25 different
vegetables, including pack-choy (pak-choi) and
celtis (celtuce). His 1966 stand also displayed
rhubarb beet (ruby chard), along with white-curded
cauliflowers and golden-ball carrots.

At the 1971 show there were floods and
thunderstorms; in 1974 the spring was advanced

only to be beaten back by late cold spells; and in
1976 everyone complained about too much sun. In
1988 the RHS began charging members to come to
Chelsea and added an extra members-only day
(Wednesday) to its now-traditional Tuesday one.
Public access to the show was therefore restricted to
Thursday and Friday.

The Chelsea Flower Show has been nurtured by
permanent uncertainty throughout its amazing run of
over 90 years. The weather is constant in its
inconstancy but, with typical British interest, the
cloudbursts and tropical sun have sometimes been
reported more than the plants. As in 1913, it is still
considered the greatest flower show on Earth. More
people want to come to it than can possibly be
accommodated, and ever more designers and
exhibitors seek to take space on its hallowed turf. It
raises huge amounts of money for charity, too. There
is nothing like it; it has no competitor.

THE ROLE OF THE ROYALS

THE WHOLE CHELSEA FLOWER SHOW is spattered with "Royal" allusions. The Royal Horticultural Society was given its first Royal charter by George III in 1809, although the word "Royal" was not added to the name until granted by Queen Victoria in 1861. It runs the show in the grounds of the Royal Hospital, Chelsea; and the Royal Family have been patrons, supporters, and assiduous visitors of the event since its inception.

The Royal Family as well as the ill-fated Archduke Franz Ferdinand of Austria and his wife, the former Bohemian Countess Sophie Chotek, visited the 1912 Royal International Horticultural Exhibition at Chelsea. Later that year the RHS Council decided that a member of the Royal Family should be invited to open the first RHS Chelsea Show, in 1913, but they left it a little late – not approaching the Duke and Duchess of Connaught until April 1913. These royals already had a prior engagement, so Queen Alexandra came, instead, on the opening day, along with Princess Victoria and the Duchess of Fife.

After a shaky start, the Royal Family has become increasingly enthusiastic about the show. Initially there was no set pattern as to which day or days they attended, but in 1920 the Royal Visits moved from public-access days to Press Day, on the Monday, to avoid the crowds. Gradually their visit – a major highlight for many exhibitors – has become bound up with the Chelsea tradition. The nurserymen and the gardeners pick tiny specks from their lawns, vacuum their sheets of water, and change from muddy dungarees to smart clothes in preparation for the reigning monarch's visit during the Monday afternoon (and, almost as important, the dark-suited judges, who are also assessing that day).

The royals have responded by becoming notably informal – though sometimes tetchy if plants were not their hobby – and by bringing along friends and foreign royals who are staying in Britain, at times in poignant circumstances. In 1919, for the first show after the First World War, Queen Alexandra brought the Empress Marie of Russia, recently deposed by the Bolsheviks. In 1922 the Queen of Spain (not yet deposed by General Franco) and her daughter were visitors; so was the Queen of Rumania (also later deposed) in 1924. The

EUROPEAN ROYALTY
Members of Royal Families from many countries support Chelsea. Here Queen Amelia of Portugal, who died in 1951, is accompanied to the 1912 Royal International Horticultural Exhibition by the Marquise de Soveral and a male escort.

Royal Party, reported the *Gardeners' Chronicle*, "asked innumerable questions and made many notes". In 1934 George V and Queen Mary brought the King and Queen of Siam and the Crown Princess of Sweden along with the Prince of Wales (later Edward VIII), and the Duke and Duchess of York (later George VI and Queen Elizabeth).

Queen Mary was an avid visitor to the show over a period of five decades. In 1939 the *Gardeners' Chronicle* reported that she had turned up despite torrents of rain, howling wind, and liquid mud underfoot, and that she had missed only one show since 1912. Her husband was far less keen on plants. In 1924, however, he developed something of an

interest in vegetables. Visiting the Hon. Vicary Gibbs's vegetable stand, displaying almost every kind of leaf or root we now eat (and a good few we do not), he asked for specimens of aubergine and the edible *Oxalis tuberosum* (now known as *O. tuberosa*) to be sent to Buckingham Palace for tasting. Yet he was clearly pretty grumpy.

In *A Wiser Woman?*, Lady Christabel Aberconway (Christabel McLaren) well recalled that frightening day "when King George was accosted by several newspaper photographers. He growled, 'This is intolerable, intolerable. They've taken quite enough photographs

DETERMINED SUPPORTER
Queen Mary (left) was an enthusiastic visitor to the Chelsea Flower Show and visited whatever the weather. Her husband, King George V (above, in 1933), did not, however, enjoy the show to the same extent as the Queen.

ROYAL VIEWS
Queen Mary (below) considers one of the show gardens at the 1938 show and (right) the cottage garden exhibit of astilbes, salvias, and helianthus, in front of an austere Pre-fab, created by the Women's Voluntary Services for Chelsea 1948.

of me today; these journalists, – I'm going back to the Palace'." Lady Christabel, obviously no soft touch, boldly reminded him that he had, after all, ennobled three press barons: Beaverbrook, Northcliffe, and Rothermere. "It was touch and go," she wrote in her memoirs. "Going through the big tent he [King George] pointed to some mauve and orange flowers placed close together. 'Horrid colours. Pink and blue, pink and blue, those are the colours that should always go together.' I then scored another mark. 'Well, sir,' I said, 'I

took my young daughter to the zoo the other day and tried to prevent her seeing certain portions of a monkey's anatomy; but she observed the creature and asked in a carrying voice, "Are those pink and blue patches meant to be the monkey's bottom?"' This delighted King George and, after that, every year he came to Chelsea he told me how much he had enjoyed that afternoon."

ACTIVE GARDENERS

Perhaps in reaction to his father's churlishness, King George's popular son Edward VIII both enjoyed and understood gardening. As Prince of Wales not only did he visit with the official Royal Party but would also return for a second look. In 1934 he purchased an entire rock garden from the show to put in his grounds at Fort Belvedere and actually helped dismantle the display.

His brother George VI and Queen

Elizabeth were also keen gardeners and fervent supporters of the show, with the King showing his own schizanthus in 1947. Denis O'Brien Baker, who exhibited at the show from 1935 to 2002, remarked, "The Queen Mother has been my favourite; she was the most interested. But I do remember seeing Queen Mary when I went to my first Chelsea as a schoolboy, in 1933."

The Duke of Gloucester was more in his father, George V's, mould. A Council member, Will Ingwersen, was showing the Duke round the marquee when he was offered a strawberry by the redoubtable Beatrix Havergal, founder of the Waterperry Horticultural School, which was known for its splendid 'Royal Sovereign' fruits. "Do you like strawberries?" the Duke of Gloucester

FAMILY OUTING
Queen Elizabeth discusses a rock garden display, while her two daughters, Princess Elizabeth and Princess Margaret, study the exhibits during the Royal Visit to the 1947 Chelsea Flower Show.

asked her. "Yes sir, don't you?" "They spoil the port," he snorted.

Faith and Geoff Whiten exhibited together for two decades and in their book, *The Chelsea Flower Show,* they recalled the day when liquid tomato fertilizer from a smashed bottle landed on the royal nylon stockings. "There was panic, confusion, sheer frozen terror ... but the royal lady herself remained charming and unruffled, though certainly surprised."

THE MONDAY RITUAL

The arrival of the Royal party is always eagerly anticipated by exhibitors and those RHS staff allowed in the grounds after the 3.30pm clearance. The scene is set, the Show is complete and at its most perfect – freshly watered so that myriad fragrances fill the marquees – and crowds are eagerly waiting outside the Bull-Ring entrance. The Royal Family arrive in

ENTHUSIASTIC VISITOR
Queen Elizabeth strides out purposefully in 1950, leaving her entourage to catch up.

reverse order of precedence, and each Royal is accompanied by a group of guests. After being greeted by the President, they set off to tour the show, guided by Council members and RHS staff – each group following a different route.

Only a few accredited photographers and other press people are allowed to stay for the Royal Visit, which has always been notably relaxed. One Council member, according to the Whitens, recalled taking Princess Alice of Athlone, a noted gardener, around the show. "Her knowledge not only of horticulture but also of many stand-holders was amazing. Consequently, after touring the show, she had collected quite a bouquet of flowers – specimens handed to her by various exhibitors. Eventually we met up with other members of the Royal Family and the Princess was asked by one, 'Auntie, where did you get that loot?' 'That

is not loot,' came the reply. 'That is floral appreciation from my friends'."

Exhibitors, however, should not have the idea that the royals discard all etiquette. One remembered how the Queen Mother refused to talk to the famous rose grower Harry Wheatcroft, because he was wearing an open-necked shirt without a tie. Nonetheless she was relaxed enough in 1980 to enjoy a Chelsea tribute to her 80th birthday by the National Farmers' Union. This was the Queen Mother's Crown, made up of a Bramley apple (*Malus domestica* 'Bramley's Seedling'), cauliflowers and strawberries. That same year the Royal Parks also exhibited a crown: it stood 20ft (6m) high and its royal purple background of African violets were some of 11,000 plants used in the whole display.

The ebb and flow of Royal family life can be followed through the official visits to

PRIVATE VIEWING
Every year there is a fine royal turnout to see the show. Prince Charles (top left) studies a show garden at the 1998 Chelsea, while the Duchess of Kent (above) saw the show at its sunny best, in 1991.

GARDENING EXPERTS

Exhibitors always said that Queen Elizabeth the Queen Mother (left, in 1971) was a highly knowledgeable gardener. Her daughter, Queen Elizabeth II (below) another garden enthusiast, holds PRIDE OF ENGLAND *('Harencore') roses presented to her in 1998 by the footballer Geoff Hurst.*

the show: in 1961 Anthony Armstrong-Jones was there with Princess Margaret and a large royal contingent; a year later he appeared as Lord Snowdon with his wife, Princess Margaret.

Amid press predictions of traffic chaos, motorcade on motorcade of royals took advantage of Chelsea's quiet afternoon to visit the 1999 show. Among the entourage were Elizabeth II and the Duke of Edinburgh (always interested in the scientific parts of the show), the Duke of York, the Duke and Duchess of Gloucester, the Duke of Kent with his daughter and her husband, Princess Alexandra and Sir Angus Ogilvy, and Princess Michael of Kent, who brought her friends along in a van. Prince Charles, the most influential gardener among the family, however was missing – he was at the Museum of Garden History across the river.

CHELSEA TODAY

"There is not a show in the world that can touch Chelsea in terms of sheer quality and spectacle."

MIXED CROWDS

Visitors to the Chelsea Flower Show are drawn from a wide range of backgrounds, even if women predominate over men by almost four to one.

WHY IS THE CHELSEA FLOWER SHOW so enormously popular? Is it because it is steeped in tradition? Or is it because this is where country meets town; where chic urbanites drink champagne and wear their designer outfits alongside elderly squires in tattered Barbours and red-faced countrywomen with muddy fingernails; where designers and architects encounter nurserymen and jobbing gardeners? Perhaps, as one exhibitor said, it is the quite indefinable thrill of being at the greatest, the best, the most prestigious flower show in the world.

To me it is all these things but, to Shows Director Stephen Bennett, it is principally the location, in the heart of London, and the time of year. "The sap's rising, gardeners are crawling out of hibernation, and it is a big buying time for plants, garden equipment, furniture, and machinery," he explained. "There is also the particular magic of the Royal Hospital site and, of course, the extraordinarily high standards of display and presentation. There is not a show in the world that can touch Chelsea in terms of sheer quality and spectacle."

Stephen Bennett and his staff behind the scenes endeavour to keep everyone at Chelsea happy. This is no easy feat when the needs of so many parties have all to be taken into account. Those involved include: exhibitors of plants, lawn mowers, conservatories, flower arrangements, and gardening magazines; the designers of the show gardens; the sponsors; the press; and, of course, the public. The site is too small; it seems always to have been too small. The demand is now so intense that since 1988 all tickets have

JOSTLING FOR POSITION

Admiring crowds still had space to move about the show relatively freely in 1951 (above) but by 1993 (right) there was much less room in which to gain a good view of a show garden.

been sold in advance to manage and control the numbers. Everyone complains constantly: the press grumbles about its ticket allocation; the public grows weary of beating sun or pelting rain and never finding enough places to sit; some exhibitors dislike the rule forbidding them to sell their plants until the end of the last day, while others object to bought-in plants rather than self-cultivated ones going on display at the show.

"Without a marketing budget, the Great Spring Flower Show became too large for three successive venues – Chiswick (1883–1887), the Inner Temple (1888–1911), and the Royal Hospital," said Bennett. "We outgrew the Royal Hospital site in the 1960s. One of the most difficult problems ... was to continue to run such a popular show on such a small site. Until 1987 it was daunting, because there was no limit on visitor numbers. We know that, in 1987, there were 247,000 visitors. There may have been even more before that but we do not have accurate numbers."

The conditions at Chelsea appalled Bennett when he arrived at the RHS in September 1985. "During my first two shows, in 1986 and 1987, I was shocked at the inconveniences endured

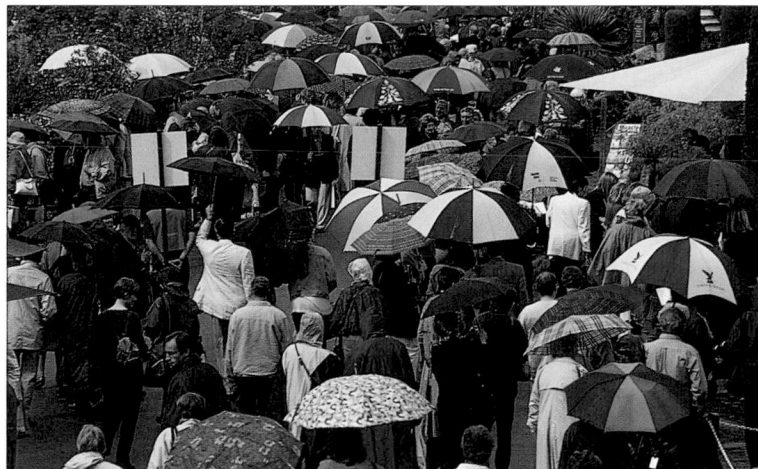

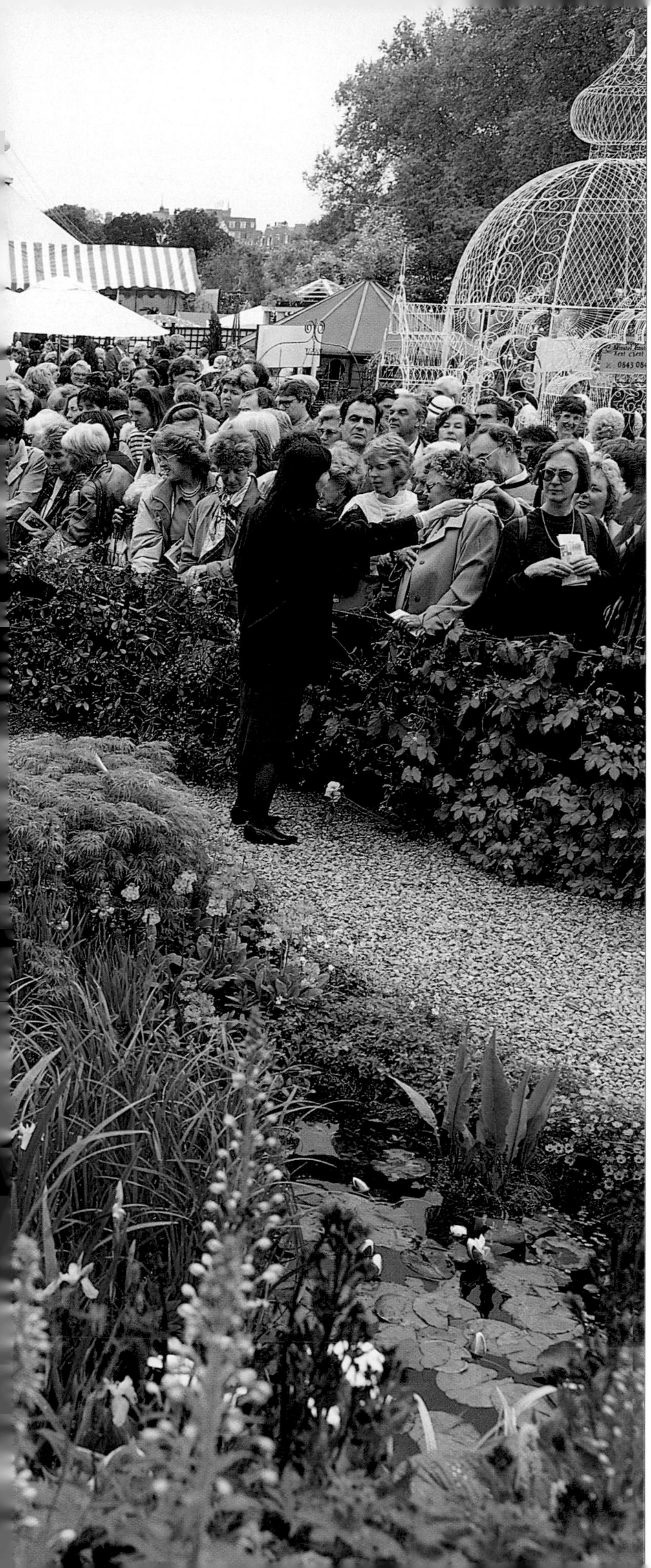

AN ENGLISH MAY DAY
The weather during Chelsea week can be very changeable, yet this rarely deters keen visitors, as seen here viewing outside stands in Southern Road at the 1997 show.

by the public. It was extremely uncomfortable and potentially dangerous. We considered moving the show. There were three options: to leave London completely; to find another venue in London – Osterley, Victoria Park, or Battersea Park all being possibilities; or to stay at Chelsea and tackle the overcrowding. We decided to take the third option, because, despite the indignities visitors suffered, everyone seemed to have an enormous affection for the Royal Hospital site. Their reasons included the uniqueness of the Wren-designed hospital building, the trees, and the Thames. The grounds have a special feel, unlike any major exhibition centre, and they are convenient for people to reach by public transport – there are taxis, Tubes, buses, and trains at nearby Victoria Station. There was a strong wish to stay."

ENHANCING CONDITIONS AT THE SHOW

The challenge was therefore to improve the comfort and safety of the visitors and exhibitors. "We decided that, in 1988, we would limit for the first time the number of visitors," continued Bennett. "We sliced off nearly 100,000, going down from around 250,000 to 160,000. At today's prices, this would have knocked

£2 million off the show revenue. Also, for the first time, we charged RHS members for their Chelsea tickets. There were protests and 10,000 members resigned in disgust, yet 20,000 joined the Society, happy to pay when they made the visit to Chelsea and content that members from further afield were no longer subsidizing the free tickets of those who lived in London. These were hugely controversial decisions but they probably saved the show. Certainly it became a safer and more enjoyable experience. One lady from the Midlands wrote, 'It's much better value now that you're charging for entrance.' I think that summed it up."

Nonetheless the RHS wanted to give its members special privileges and so, since 1988, only

members are allowed into the show on Tuesday and Wednesday, with ticket prices currently from around £9 to £25, while the general public is confined to Thursday and Friday and pays from £13 to £30. Bennett believed that, if non-members were allowed in on Tuesday and Wednesday, tickets would be at least £40 for the first day and the RHS would make even more profit on the show. The challenge in ticket pricing is to strike a balance between members' privileges and optimizing income.

Since that important decision in 1988, the RHS has also begun to satisfy a growing demand by becoming involved in shows elsewhere in London and around the country. They stage a big spring show in Malvern in early May and BBC *Gardeners' World Live* in Birmingham in mid-June, followed by the Society's biggest show – at Hampton Court Palace – in early July and the RHS show at Tatton Park, Cheshire, later the same month. The Scottish show, held at Strathclyde Country Park from 1997 to 1999, was cancelled after its three-year run. "We had hoped to build a major event with an attendance that would at least cover the costs of staging the show," said Bennett. A press release summed up the

CHANGING TRENDS
In the 1980s, when conservatories became fashionable, the RHS struggled to meet demands for more space by their manufacturers, who wished to exhibit their bulky products, preferably in a suitably attractive setting.

situation. "Sadly the level of support from the Scottish gardening public has fallen short of expectation and, having subsidized the show for three years, the Society has now decided with regret not to run the show in Strathclyde. It was influenced in its decision by declining support for the show from the non-floral exhibitors." Alternative events might some time be launched in Scotland, but the demise of Strathclyde illustrates the financial risk involved in putting on a major show.

The RHS has acquired other benefits by moving out of the home counties. Bennett believed that "there is huge potential for increasing membership in the regions, and membership produces the steadiest source of income. We need to have a strong presence outside south-east England, and we aim to have

shows at different times of the year for plants such as fruit, vegetables, and dahlias, which attract both amateurs and professionals. Chelsea is not much good for growers of these plants. Of course it is not only the RHS that can provide such shows: there are already thousands of small and several big ones such as those at Harrogate, Ayr, Shrewsbury, Holker Hall, and Southport, and we try to avoid the dates clashing. The RHS has established the standards and the important principle that we do not allow plants to be sold at our shows without a visual contribution. Without this policy you would end up with a street market atmosphere with no educational value." This principle is taken to extremes at Chelsea. Plants may not be sold from the stands until an hour before the whole show closes. Other shows are less stringent –

△ RUBUS TRIDEL
'BENENDEN'
(now known as Rubus 'Benenden')
Award of Merit 1957
Exhibited by Capt Collingwood
Ingram.

◁ WHERE TO SIT?
From the first Chelsea, visitors have complained that there are never enough seats on which to take a much-needed rest, but the organizers have worked hard to overcome this situation.

Chelsea can only remain at the top by constant vigilance and that is Bennett's responsibility. "We need to be very careful with our policies, because some nursery exhibitors, having tasted the benefits of selling elsewhere, are now demanding that facility for Chelsea. It's a very tricky question. There are practical constraints. The site is not big enough to accommodate the storage and access that a large demand for plants would create. We would have to lose about a third of the exhibitors in the pavilion. Local authorities, overseas exhibitors, charities, and botanic gardens, none of whom want to sell, would be under threat and their removal would be damaging for the show as a whole. Nor do all the nurseries want to sell. Many use Chelsea to promote their businesses and would be disturbed by the introduction of retail plants on neighbouring stands. It would be a distraction and would change the chemistry of the show."

RETAIL SPACE AT CHELSEA

The next decision for Bennett could be whether to make a separate retail section elsewhere in the grounds – a plant market in Ranelagh Gardens, for example. "We could insist that everyone in the plant market must also be in the Great Chelsea Pavilion. The problem here is that 90 per cent of the exhibitors are small businesses – husband-and-wife teams who grow, load, drive, stage, man, and dismantle their own stands. We know from the examples in the past at Harrogate and Shrewsbury, both of which used to split up the selling and display areas, that the exhibitors found the plant market was where the money was, not in the marquees. Displays were abandoned and the real educational value of the show dislocated."

and this is yet another reason why Chelsea is such a great spectacle. "We established the criteria, and these policies have lifted standards," Bennett went on. "It's no secret that Chelsea has always been the benchmark – and still is in terms of quality." Exhibitors agree: an RHS Gold Medal at Chelsea is the equivalent of winning at Wimbledon.

"Chelsea's reputation as the world's premier show, elite and exclusive, has been enhanced by all this," Bennett said. "The awards are displayed with pride. For the world's media and visitors alike, it towers above others for its sheer impact and quality."

EXOCHORDA X
MACRANTHA 'THE BRIDE'
First Class Certificate 1985
Exhibited by Crown Estate,
Windsor.

Other problems that arise at Chelsea are caused by changing fashions. Since the 1980s, when conservatories became very popular, there has been a big demand for show space by their manufacturers. There has also been pressure for more room by firms selling powered machinery – lawn mowers and twig shredders, strimmers, and powered scythes. By contrast, the desire for space from the local authorities has declined, because so many parks are now privatized and the new private firms feel no need to boast of their bedding schemes.

The rising demand from the manufacturers of big, expensive items is fuelled by Chelsea's many rich customers. Bennett however noted, "We are very careful to encourage people who are keen gardeners. Chelsea is not a family day out and we take care in targeting the gardening market. There is no discount for children, no family tickets, no children's play areas. Exhibitors want customers and our job is to manage the balance between the needs of exhibitors and those of the visitors. It's important to have the right number of exhibitors in each category with a good range of prices, from expensive to economic. We try to pick those with good after-sales service. If we discover a rogue exhibitor – and it has happened once or twice – we swiftly replace them."

"Every year we study the problem areas and try to enhance the show," added Chelsea Show Exhibitor Manager Mavis Sweetingham (now retired). "We look at the toilets and the catering; we endeavour to improve the facilities for disabled visitors. At the end of every show, we have a long debriefing session to identify where we had difficulties that we can alleviate."

In general the crowds and the exhibitors stay good-humoured. "People seem to be happy. We see very few arguments and tempers rarely flare," said Mavis Sweetingham, "although the Sunday and Monday before the show opens can be very fraught." Until the judging is finished, exhibitors guard their stands like tigers, shooing away intrusive journalists and TV stars with orders to stay off the grass. They and the RHS staff each year strive to make the show better, and so enable the RHS President to announce at the opening lunch for the press, "This is the best Chelsea ever."

PRESSURE FOR SPACE

Heavy machinery firms would like to have even more space in which to display their bulky goods to Chelsea's discerning gardeners, but their demands only add to the overcrowding problems at the showground.

STARTLING STATISTICS

I LOVE STATISTICS, even though they can be used to prove almost anything. Thus, in an exhibitor list handed out to the press, the RHS entitled Chelsea "The world's greatest living masterpiece". The Chelsea Flower Show certainly excels in all sorts of ways – not least in the number of superlatives that it seems to attract.

It is the first event of the London Season, and its Gala Preview is perhaps the biggest annual fund-raising event in Britain. Nearly 250,000 people thronged into the 1987 Chelsea Flower Show, and this was considered so risky that visitors are now limited. Of the 160,000 people who manage to buy tickets, along with the exhibitors, contractors, and officials, about 17,000 are from overseas. Often, the entire security force seems to have come from South Africa, and there was also a dazzling selection of jet-setters at the Gala Preview.

The RHS believe that exhibitors spend, in total, an estimated £20 million on their displays, which survive only five days – from the Royal Visit and Press Day on the Monday to the show's break up on the following Friday. As Shows Director Stephen Bennett commented, "The cost of creating a garden display can range from £40,000 to £200,000 and can take the best part of a year in blood, sweat, and tears." More than a thousand press, TV, and radio journalists from around the world report on this amazing event.

The RHS has also assessed who comes to Chelsea. The vast majority are British: 89 per cent of the total. More than half of these are from south-east England. So those who live in the capital, or within approximately three hours of London account for around fifty six percent, or six in

OVERCROWDING ▷
The show attracts more than 40,000 daily visitors, but despite the congestion Chelsea tickets are among the most sought-after of any major horticultural event in the world.

△ CHAMPAGNE GALORE
Probably more champagne is drunk in a shorter time at Chelsea's Gala Preview than at any other charity event held regularly in Britain. Here, in 1997, the caterers prepare for the celebrity guests, who vie to attend such a fashionable event.

◁ MUSIC FOR THE MEDIA
Eleven per cent of visitors to Chelsea are from overseas, and many countries exhibit at the show. To attract attention, stands for such tourist spots as the Caribbean bring in steel bands for entertainment on Press Day.

every ten visitors. The remaining twenty eight per cent of British visitors are from the further reaches of the UK, that is the south-west, the Midlands, Yorkshire & Humberside, the north, and the north-west counties of England, Scotland, Wales and Northern Ireland combined.

Twice as many visitors arrive from overseas than from East Anglia or the South West of England (at five per cent each). Unsurprisingly, the largest percentage of regional visitors come from London, at thirty six per cent, followed by the southern and south eastern counties at ten per cent each. The total number of overseas visitors to Chelsea is eleven per cent, with many of those originating from as far away as New Zealand and Australia.

As might be expected, most visitors tend to be middle aged. Of course, the price of the tickets, the ability to take time off during the week, and the sheer tradition of the event make it less enticing for trendy young urbanites or those too poor to contemplate up-market gardening shows. Even so, 25 per cent of visitors are aged 55–64 and 25 per cent aged 45–54, while 24 per cent are in the 35–44 age group. More surprisingly no fewer than 11 per cent are aged 16–34 (one per

SENIOR SHOWGOER

*RHS statistics reveal that more than
half of the total number of visitors to
Chelsea are aged 45 years or more.*

cent of these being between 16 and 24) and 15 per cent are 65 plus. The split between the sexes is an extraordinary 66 per cent female, 34 per cent male.

Each show takes 18 months to organize and three weeks to install, at a total cost of about £3.5 million. Some 2½ miles (4km) of heavy electric cable is threaded under the site along with 5 miles (8km) of water pipes. Some of these are for the 200-plus toilets destined to cope with the onrush of visitors.

A RECORD IN CANVAS

The Great Marquee itself merited a few statistics, although 1999 was its last year. As the biggest in the world, and covering 3.4 acres (1.4 hectares) of ground, it entered *The Guinness Book of Records*. The walls and roof needed 6.8 acres (2.8 hectares) of canvas. The thick thread that held the whole together would have stretched the 274 miles (440km) from London to Newcastle-upon-Tyne. It weighed more than 65 tons and took 20 men more than 19 days to erect. The last Great Marquee was 13 years old and was the fourth to be built since 1951. The supporting structure, however, had remained the same throughout these five decades. Once the show was over, the marquee was divided into 512 separate strips of canvas. These were then cleaned, checked, and repaired, before being carefully wrapped and securely stored for the following year.

The amount of food and drink demolished during show week is considerable. The Chelsea Flower Show 2001 sales analysis recorded that

AWE-INSPIRING ACRES

*The enormous size of the Great Marquee,
the biggest area of canvas in the world,
could best be appreciated when it was empty
of plants, stands, and visitors.*

some 6,500 bottles of champagne – most of the last being served to over 7,000 guests at the Gala Preview – more champagne than at any other regular party in the UK.

These 5,000 special visitors at the Gala Preview are looked after by 32 on-site catering managers controlling 424 waiting staff. The rest of the show involves 35 managers, 60 chefs, 154 waiting staff and 179 service staff as well as 69 porters and 52 other helpers. The Chelsea Flower Show is therefore a major catering operation by any standard.

SUMMER REFRESHMENT
One of the most popular rest areas at the show are the special bars that serve Pimm's – that deceptively light cocktail, with its traditional garnish of cucumber, mint, lemon, and borage flowers.

around 46,000 servings of ice cream are eaten, along with more than 5,000 servings of fish and chips. More than 21,000 pieces of cake are consumed as well as 20,000 rounds of sandwiches and 8,000 baguettes. No fewer than 43,000 cups of tea and coffee are drunk, as well as 11,000 gallons of fresh orange juice and 55,000 other cold drinks. Visitors also imbibe around 8,000 bottles of wine, 18,000 glasses of Pimm's and consume

FINANCIAL FACTS

THE ROYAL HORTICULTURAL SOCIETY is Britain's greatest gardening charity. At the height of excitement over new plant introductions from all over the world, the Society began life, in 1804, in a room above Hatchard's bookshop in Piccadilly, central London. The explorer-botanist Sir Joseph Banks and John Wedgwood (son of Josiah Wedgwood, the potter) were among its founders, and the Society's aims were to collect information about all plants and to encourage better horticultural practice. Its first show, from which all others were to develop, was a floral fête in Chiswick in the late 1820s.

Since then the Society has so grown that, despite being based on a small island, it is now the world's leading horticultural organization, active in plant collection, horticultural science, and passing on its knowledge through education. This does not come cheaply.

The Society currently spends £27 million each year to fulfil its charitable objectives. Its financial commitments include scientific and educational research, field trials, maintenance of four gardens (at Wisley in Surrey, Rosemoor in Devon, Hyde Hall in Essex and Harlow Carr in North Yorkshire), and the production of its specialist publications that are so essential to horticultural science and education but are not commercially viable. It also finances a seed distribution scheme for its members, whereby the seeds of 900 plants are harvested each year and sent throughout the world in some 250,000 seed packets. In addition the RHS advisory service offers free expert horticultural advice to members, roughly 30,000 of which use its helpline each year.

The eight RHS London shows held at the Royal Horticultural Halls, Westminster, are not self funding and rely heavily on society funding, as does the Lindley Library. This temporarily closed in 1999 so that it could be rehoused at the end of 2001 in conditions far superior to the charming but cramped ones it endured on the third floor of the Society's Vincent Square offices. The new library boasts not only vastly improved facilities for the conservation of the society's valuable collections of rare botanical books and art, but also impressive research

BALANCING THE BOOKS
Most Chelsea exhibitors such as this one selling the latest lawn tractors and other powered machinery offset the cost of their sites by taking orders for delivery after the show has closed.

TELEVISION TIE-IN
While exhibitors in the main marquees and educational areas are charged nothing for their stands, sundriesmen such as Whichford Pottery pay a fee to the RHS. In their stand for 1996 they re-created the children's television characters Bill and Ben the flowerpot men.

amenities for the public. Most of my research for this book was done in the old library, daily visited by many keen gardeners, researchers, and scholars. It was and still is a unique resource and open free to everyone, not just RHS members.

A major contribution towards these charitable works comes from the members' subscriptions. There are currently more than 330,000 members, and numbers are rising steadily. Another source of revenue is the RHS shows. Despite being extremely costly to stage every year, Chelsea has generally made an annual profit. "But," says Shows Director Stephen Bennett, "it is by no means an easy or sure way to make money."

"When other organizations hear that Chelsea makes a profit they all want to start their own shows," comments Bennett, "and there has been a plethora of new ones in the

FLORAL DISPLAYS FOR FREE ▷
Professional florists and amateur flower arrangers (shown here in 1993) are among the beneficiaries of the Society's no-charge policy for Chelsea floral stands.

▽ FLOWER FASHIONS
Exhibits at Chelsea (here in 1994) chart the changing styles of floral arrangements as well as the blooms that are in vogue.

past ten or 15 years. Most of which have either flopped immediately or failed slowly. New shows rarely make a profit in their first five years, and many of them have to be supported by horticultural or agricultural societies. It took five years for our show at Hampton Court to make a cumulative contribution. It is because Chelsea has such immense pulling power that it can deliver a profit."

GEUM 'LADY
STRATHEDEN'
Award of Merit 1920

Much of the profit, however, is now being ploughed back into the show as investment in its future, and the cost of the latest changes, including the replacement of the marquee, has reduced profit dramatically. Stephen Bennett explains, "Commissioning the new design, the construction of the new superstructure, and all the associated work are, of course, one-off costs. Now it's up, however, it will cost more each year to hire than the old Great Marquee did. We could, of course, have bought a new canvas marquee, as before. That would have been cheaper but it was outdated in its materials, fireproofing, and flexibility ... the advantages of the new structure are that it is higher, bigger, better-ventilated, and safer."

As a charity, the RHS does not ask certain exhibitors to pay for their Chelsea stands. Among those that benefit are the show garden sites and the exhibitors of plants in what was the Great Marquee. Such

◁ MONEY-MAKING MERCHANDISE
*Big garden-building and conservatory companies, such as Marston &
Langinger here in 1999, regularly put on fine displays at the Chelsea Show.*

exhibitors may make their names and, perhaps, their fortunes from exposure at Chelsea but the site is free. Nor do any of the following have to rent their spaces at the show: the fruit, flower, and vegetable exhibitors; the educational and scientific groups; the florists and floral-arranging exhibitors; those who enter their window boxes and hanging baskets (which moved to the Hampton Court show in 2000); the designers of courtyard gardens; and the garden designers themselves. Thus, those 180-odd horticultural stands in the tents, the show gardens, and the amateur and professional societies have free sites, although their exhibits are frequently expensive to stage.

Some companies do have to pay for their sites. These are generally those that sell direct to the public from their stands – something that the other exhibitors are not able to do (although, of course, they can take orders to be delivered later). Those charged include: companies selling heavy machinery such as lawn tractors, lawn mowers, watering systems, and hedge clippers; those who exhibit conservatories; and other firms who sell smaller tools, forks, aprons, and secateurs, directly over the counter. Stalls that sell gardening books, magazines, and sundries are also charged to be at the Chelsea Flower Show. It seems fair enough and these firms, too, clamour for the limited space. "The RHS provides a platform for the exhibitors to excite and interest the public," concluded Bennett. "It is the Royal Horticultural Society seen publicly at its best."

ROLE REVERSAL
*While some commercial exhibitors dress up
their stands with human-looking pots or
vegetables, other stands may feature humans
disguised as statues.*

BEHIND THE SCENES

"The point about Chelsea is that, if there's a problem, every single person will turn out to help."

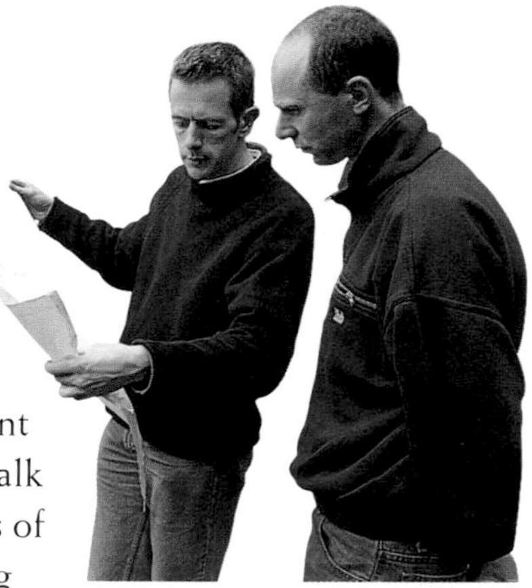

DESIGN BRAINSTORM *Stephen Woodhams (left) discusses his plans for restaurateur "Sally Clarke's Kitchen Garden", in 1996.*

THE FIRST ON-SITE JOB at the Chelsea showground is just as traditional as the rest of the event. Members of the RHS Shows Department and the Lieutenant Governor of the Royal Hospital walk around the whole site, checking for signs of damage, as one would on taking possession of a hire car. What is found to be blemished during the walk is the Royal Hospital's affair; what is damaged during the days and nights that follow is the Society's responsibility. When the state of the ground is agreed, both parties shake hands and the deal is done for another year. Nobody really expects the handshake to be withheld (and luckily it never has been), since the RHS Shows staff have already been around the ground, spraying the grass with semi-permanent paint to delineate the sites of the marquees and tents, the exhibitor stands, courtyard and show gardens, the conservatories and glasshouses, the toilets, and the restaurants.

Handover always happens on a Monday morning, 21 days before Press Day and the Royal Visit to the show. In these three weeks, the picturesque grounds of the Royal Hospital with their mature trees and open spaces are transformed into the complex showground of the world's most prestigious flower show. Obviously there's no time to be wasted, so, immediately the handshake is made, the RHS Shows Department thunders into action. At about midday the security guards arrive together with CCTV cameras, gate padlocks are changed, and portable cabins complete with power and telephone links are installed. The cabins, positioned at the Bull-Ring Gate entrance, will become "homes"

◁ FINISHING TOUCHES *Ridging tiles are positioned on a timber roof.*

ROSA POLAR STAR
('Tanlarpost')
Rose of the Year 1985

MARVELLOUS MACHINES
*Heavy diggers, as here in 1997,
make construction of the show
gardens much easier than at early
shows, which relied on men using
mattocks and spades.*

to the Chelsea Operations Manager, Chelsea Show Exhibitor Manager, and their assistants for the whole period of the show, from the build-up right through to the breakdown.

The Society's contractors are at work, too, carefully removing tons of topsoil from the rock garden bank and piling it up behind 330ft (100m) of cladded scaffold, which acts both as a retaining wall and screen. In addition to this, a second scaffolded area of some 200ft (60m), next to the Ambulance Gate, has been taken over to hide extra topsoil, which will of course be put back in its original place after the show. Drains and manholes are covered with metal plates; kerbs are protected using hundreds of railway sleepers and tarmac ramps, installed in various strategic places to help access for vehicles, pedestrians, and wheelchairs. Hundreds of yards of metal and plastic temporary trackway are laid to

form new roads and paths, so the grounds are shielded against construction traffic.

During the first week of the build-up, the RHS staff are also tidying up. They mow the grass and prune and shield from damage any fragile or awkward trees. One tree in particular is protected by law: the exhibitor manual states that, while no trees must be damaged, exhibitors on Main Avenue whose gardens adjoin a *Liriodendron* tree (marked on the plan they receive) must ensure that excavations and heavy materials are kept as far as possible away from the timber tree guards to avoid damaging the roots.

Other rules and regulations are also clearly laid out in this hefty exhibitor manual, which is distributed to contractors, exhibitors, and designers. In addition, and in order to meet health and safety requirements at shows, the RHS has created a special booklet specific to each show,

PLANT PARADE

A gang of gardeners, some in traditional flat caps and overalls or dungarees, carry their precious exhibits into the Royal Hospital grounds, in 1955.

which is sent to everyone affected. Contractors are firmly told that they will not be given the relevant badges and passes unless they have completed and returned all health and safety forms. Forklift trucks, diggers, dumpers, and articulated lorries are all driven on to the site, and with such a high level of construction activity such controls are badly needed. "We can fine anyone who causes reckless damage," said former Operations Manager, Nick Yarsley, adding that they have not yet been forced to do so.

Over the weeks of the build-up, there are some 16,000 movements of vehicles. This horrific traffic scenario requires careful monitoring, so the

EARTHWORKS
Tons of soil are removed to behind cladded scaffold every year in the run-up to Chelsea, to accommodate the show gardens, and it is then put back and reseeded once the show has closed.

CONSTRUCTION TEAM
Gardeners help build the Evening Standard's 1997 show garden, "Classical Calm with a Touch of Tomorrow", which was designed by Xa Tollemache.

contractors' access into the site is minutely planned. In a typical year, exhibitors begin the build-up in early May, with the show gardens being given the most generous times for their major works. Their contractors are allowed into the grounds from 7am, and told to be completely finished by 7.30am some 19 days later, around 24 May. Because of ever-increasing interest from the press and TV within the showground on the Sunday before opening, the manual now warns that it is better if work is finished by the Sunday, rather than the Monday.

Until Chelsea 2000, the largest contractor was Piggotts Bros, who arrived to put up the canvas Great Marquee. In the past their experienced workmen would immediately begin exposing some 130 or so drainage ducts hidden beneath the grass, into which the marquee drainage posts would be slotted. "There were never less than 12 men at work," explained Yarsley, "and the methods of erecting the marquee's canvas hadn't changed much since the first one went up many decades ago. It was all a matter of ropes, posts, pulleys, and sweat – a bit like being on a ship. Whereas forklifts may be used for carrying the large poles around, they are not too practical when it comes to lifting the delicate canvas; that is still best done by hand."

As the Great Marquee began to rise, after its year-long hibernation, other large tents started to appear. There was a two-tier restaurant for visitors, 16 chalets complete with a kitchen for the corporate hospitality village, a canteen for exhibitors and contractors (as well as staff), and office tents for the various RHS departments that decamp to the site for the show. There is also an airy Press tent complete with racks for exhibitors' press releases, tables and chairs for weary journalists, and a TV for viewing the daily live coverage of the show. In addition the Press tent has an outdoor veranda from which media stars can watch the crowds in splendid isolation.

Scaffolding is erected to support catering tents that have to be positioned on uneven ground. One structure is under a visitors' restaurant that has superb views of both the Thames and the show, while the other is under the large exhibitors' restaurant in Ranelagh Gardens. Scaffolding is also vital throughout the show for carrying electrical, telephone, and TV cables, as well as water pipes. Emergency exit signs, banners, and the PA system are all suspended using scaffold towers. The Bull-Ring Gate also has a large scaffold built around it. "The gate is an antique and was never designed for flower shows," Yarsley commented ruefully. "It's very narrow and unfortunately English Heritage won't let us widen it so we have to try to protect it. We use scaffolding and timber sheeting not only to protect it but also to create a smart bespoke entrance for the show."

Large green plastic sheeting is hung all along the Embankment railings. This is not, as I had

BUILDING FROM SCRATCH

Vast quantities of garden impedimenta are trucked into the Chelsea site during the three-week run-up to the show, but, by the time the awards are announced on the opening Tuesday, all is in pristine order.

imagined, to stop the public peeking in but to hide the "mess" of construction inside the showground. Such sheeting is also often required throughout the show to conceal the many unsightly areas from the visitor. Miles of water pipe are laid throughout the site each year, and these link into two 20,000 gallon (90,000 litres) water tanks, which supply all the site's needs – from the plants themselves to the toilets. Before the show, huge quantities of electrical cables are constantly being unrolled, for the catering, lighting, offices, exhibits, and additional generators. "Every year people try harder to outdo each other, which has a knock-on effect," explained Yarsley. Recently, the

GLIMPSE OF THE PAST
On the far side of a Chinese-inspired moon gate, workmen build a fountain in a show garden for the 1949 Chelsea Flower Show.

The RHS tries to look after the disabled, too. "We have someone who comes every year to inspect our facilities. She has a very critical eye. We try hard to provide decent ramps, handrails, and friendly access points, but are often restricted financially or by what is actually available to hire. In particular I have found it hard to find disabled toilets that meet with all the respective guidelines. Five years ago I had one block custom-built," said Yarsley gleefully. "I believe this was well received and seen as a significant step forward, so I am now obviously keen that we should progress this for future shows."

Heavy digging and foundation laying for the show gardens may take most of the first two weeks but, by the third week, plants are starting to appear. Firms exhibiting "sundries" on open-ground plots begin to bring in their lawn mowers, tractors, cultivators, furniture, pottery, statues, and sculptures, and the conservatories look almost habitable.

With only a week before the show opens, other exhibitors start to arrive. Work begins on the smaller gardens, and the majority of exhibitors in the Great Pavilion move in to transform the bleak structure into an astonishing unseasonal floral paradise. Some exhibitors work right through the night to complete their spectaculars on time.

Imagine those last few days, when the build-up really gains momentum. "Once the construction vehicles have departed, hundreds of smaller vehicles move in: box vans, horseboxes, estate cars, and trailers. It's like a one-way M25 car park!" continued Yarsley. "The last weekend, starting on the Friday, is

television coverage required a double-deck studio for live broadcasts, four camera crews, numerous offices, production vehicles, and even a crane for aerial shots, all of which needed a great deal of electrical power.

MEETING AN EVER-INCREASING DEMAND

Then there are growing requests for restaurant places. "We are putting in more seats and facilities all the time. Ten years ago, when I first worked on Chelsea, I was surprised to see elderly ladies dressed in their best, sitting on kerbs eating their sandwiches. It didn't seem quite right to me, so we took immediate steps to improve matters," reflected Yarsley.

The RHS also constructs three ladies' blocks, each with 40 toilets and hand basins, a gents' block, and a tailor-made disabled unit. "Although we install more toilets than are required under the government guidelines we still suffer from queues, as for some strange reason visitors always seem to go at the same time," Yarsley commented. "In 1999 we purchased two new cubicle blocks, which cost £50,000, and that did not include fittings or installation costs. In addition to these 'fixed' facilities we bring in mobile units, which each year increase in number."

TIME FOR A PAUSE

Michael Miller (left) considers his "Classical Garden" for 1994, which was sponsored by Cartier and Harpers & Queen. It was based on the French formal gardening tradition.

FINAL COUNTDOWN ▷

On Day 1 of erecting the 1994 "Classical Garden" at Chelsea: wiring and water pumps were installed. Day 2: pits for six 20-year-old pleached limes were excavated. Day 3: a trench for a 12ft (4m) yew was dug. Days 4–10: an historically correct arbour was built and a canal made. Days 11–14: large shrubs were planted, heavy yew trees raised on crates to give an illusion of height, and box parterre hedges inched into place. Days 15–17: lavender, sage, and allium were planted. Days 18–19: lawns were turfed and the canal filled with water.

ROCKS AND ROCK GARDENS

Huge rocks have featured in many gardens at Chelsea. Originally they were brought in by horses and manoeuvred by hand, but they are now delivered by forklifts and moved by cranes, as they were for Douglas G. Knight's "Rock and Waterfall Garden" in 1997, which is, here, being planted up.

certain that the ladies' toilets are finished, complete with cheval mirrors. "One year they were forgotten; the complaints were unbelievable," remarked Yarsley.

As the weekend chaos subsides, some areas are cleaned up in time for the few privileged members of the public and press who arrive for Build-Up Sunday. Other parts of the show are ready only in time for the Monday – the main Press Day – when judging takes place and the Gala Preview is held in the evening, amid well-upholstered chairs and special decorations. All of these are moved before members' day on the Tuesday, when the show gates open in earnest. The exhibitors who were sweaty and covered in soil on Sunday are now in smart clothes, and the Gold Medals and other awards, decided

the busiest. We're bringing in thousands of seats for the restaurants, public areas, and the offices." On the Friday, too, the firms in the "shell-scheme stands" arrive to stage their exhibits of garden tools, paintings, books, magazines, terracotta pots, equipment, and all types of interesting gardening gadgets. These specially constructed stands – originally adapted from an indoor system – stretch for some 1.2 miles (2km). Over the last weekend the only other exhibits to enter the showground are the floristry, floral arrangers, window box and hanging basket displays, and the senior and junior garden exhibits.

"A few days before we open we're virtually on top, with the last couple of days used for the fine tuning," Yarsley explained. Fine tuning by the RHS staff may include making

LAST MANICURE

Many nurserymen design their stands by eye once they arrive at the showground, while others carefully follow detailed pre-conceived plans. Here an exhibitor puts the finishing touches to his rhododendron display, before the 1994 show officially opens.

only on the Monday night, are prominently positioned. For a brief four days, visitors stroll around the show. The roses bloom immaculately, and the show gardens draw cries of admiration.

Then, at 4.30pm on the Friday, a bell is rung and the demolition begins: the plants are wrenched from the stands and sold at an auctioneer's pace. The weary exhibitors queue in the New Covent Garden Market before being allowed to bring back their vans, estate cars, and horseboxes and pack everything up again. Heavy cranes and forklifts arrive in droves ready for their destructive tasks. Gardens that took two and a half weeks to build come apart in as many days; the Great Marquee,

which needed nearly three weeks to erect, was down in less than five days before it became obsolete in 2000. The new structure takes 25 days to assemble and 9 to dismantle. The remaining challenge for the RHS Shows Department staff is to return the site to its pristine Royal Hospital self.

"It all depends on the weather," explained Yarsley. "If it is bad, it is hell. The site sometimes resembles a bomb site."

Eventually, though, the grounds are cleared of tents, scaffolding is struck, the waste removed, the precious topsoil returned to its rightful place, and the area reseeded with grass. Within a further few weeks, another Chelsea has become just a memory.

RURAL RETREAT
In his Country Life *"Centenary Garden" in 1997, Rupert Golby included a wild area with an old tree trunk – as a haven for insects – and sculptured sheep by Rupert Till, as well as an old shed for a sheep shelter.*

UNDER CANVAS

AS I LEFT THE GREAT MARQUEE in the final hour of the final day of the 1999 Chelsea Flower Show, I patted the tired old canvas, no longer pristine white but dull and, here and there, frayed. Every May, for 13 years, it had withstood some extreme weather – gales, thunderstorms, heatwaves, and hailstones – within the Royal Hospital grounds and had become a friend to me and thousands of other keen visitors to the show.

Unfortunately I would never again see this particular old friend. It was – for me – a sad parting. I knew that by the next show the greatest marquee in the world would have been replaced by the high-tech Floral Pavilions.

Until 1999 the RHS had owned a succession of marquees, which had been erected by Piggotts Bros, except just occasionally – as in the early 1920s – when competitors had done the job more cheaply. Although these marquees had frequently changed in shape and size, they had always been made and erected with 19th-century technology. Piggotts, working from a Victorian workhouse in Ongar on the outskirts of London, had originally made canvas sails for the Royal Navy and duck tents for the Army, when whole regiments would live under canvas during such conflicts as the Crimean War. The huge marquees, sewn by treadle sewing machines for successive Chelsea shows, were an extension of this type of work.

Initially there was only one comparatively small marquee, but in 1924 two were needed to contain all the exhibits. They became known as the East Marquee and the West

HIDDEN VISTA
From 1951 until the Floral Pavilions were introduced in 2000, the view of Sir Christopher Wren's Royal Hospital was obscured by vast expanses of white canvas.

◁ **A SENSITIVE TOUCH**
Machinery was too rough to handle the fragile canvas, so the Great Marquee had to be hauled into position using manual labour, as here in 1960.

**HEMEROCALLIS
'STELLA DE ORO'**
First Class Certificate 1985

Marquee. In 1951, again to ease pressure on space within the covered area of the show, the two marquees were joined to make the Great Marquee. This was the biggest marquee in the world; even at the time of its demise, in 1999, it remained so. The Great Marquee was so large that it had no other use – no one else wanted it. From one Chelsea Flower Show to the next it was taken to pieces, and stored at Ongar in specially made canvas bags.

The Great Marquee was, in fact, a series of nine joined-up tents, each of which had its apex above a line of exhibitors. Between each apex was a pedestrian aisle, at the low point of each tent. The whole marquee had 278 supports, half of them Queen poles for the apexes and half of them stubbier poles for the valleys, from which rainwater was conducted into the drainage system, which used the River Thames as its final outlet.

"Piggotts had been making the tents since 1913," explained Shows Director Stephen Bennett. "They were of cotton duck canvas, which was good, clean, and light, and had a life of about ten years. Actually each marquee has done more than ten years

– anything between 12 and 14. One of the problems has always been that, as it aged, the canvas discoloured and, for plants, light is important. They need good quality, white light, so we decided that the canvas had to be replaced … The infrastructure was also fraying, the posts, block and tackle, and ropes were ancient, and the timber poles were rotting away. Had we put up the Great Marquee on a new site, we'd never have got permission because of the fire regulations."

To meet current fire regulations an entirely different scheme was devised, using modern materials. "The RHS had a choice between clear-span aluminium tentage, which is the dull but cheap option," Bennett explained, "or a tri-dimensional structure with modules of 80ft (25m) by 70ft (20m), which could be rearranged every year. This would be of steel with a clean, white, PVC top." The Society went for the more expensive – but much more exciting – choice only a month before 1999 Chelsea opened and when plans were already quite advanced for the following year.

As well as providing better light and

SETTING THE RIGGING

The long experience that Piggotts gained from supplying Royal Naval ships with canvas sails proved invaluable when erecting the vast marquees for Chelsea.

PROBLEM RESOLVED

Many nurserymen chose to decorate the numerous poles within the Great Marquee with climbers or trees, and thus transform them into an asset within their display.

ventilation than the Great Marquee, the number of poles in the new Pavilion has been dramatically reduced. The flexibility of the new scheme was even more important. Each module can be positioned in a different format every year with, excitingly, the possibility of opening some exhibitors' space to the elements. Thus some show gardens, which traditionally

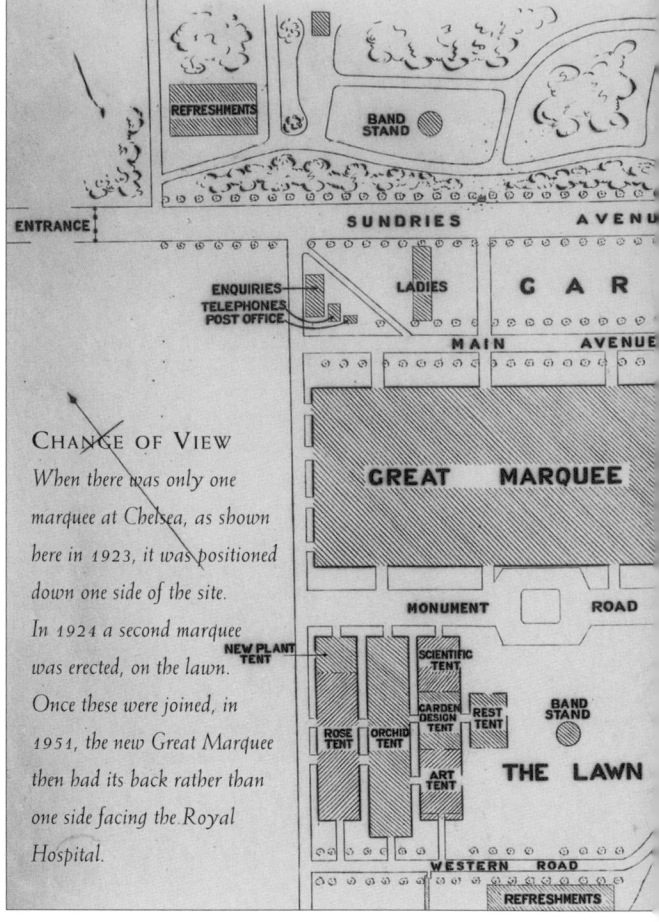

CHANGE OF VIEW
When there was only one marquee at Chelsea, as shown here in 1923, it was positioned down one side of the site. In 1924 a second marquee was erected, on the lawn. Once these were joined, in 1951, the new Great Marquee then had its back rather than one side facing the Royal Hospital.

had been in the open air, can now be interspersed with the exhibits that were under canvas.

From 2000 to 2003, the new structure was divided into two pavilions and while this layout caused some loss in the continuity of exhibits, it had the advantage of opening up a stunning vista from the Thames to the splendid architecture of Sir Christopher Wren's Royal Hospital, which is one of the site's main attributes (see illustration on opposite page).

However, a decision was made to revert to one structure in 2004, which has taken in the central broad alley and posed the

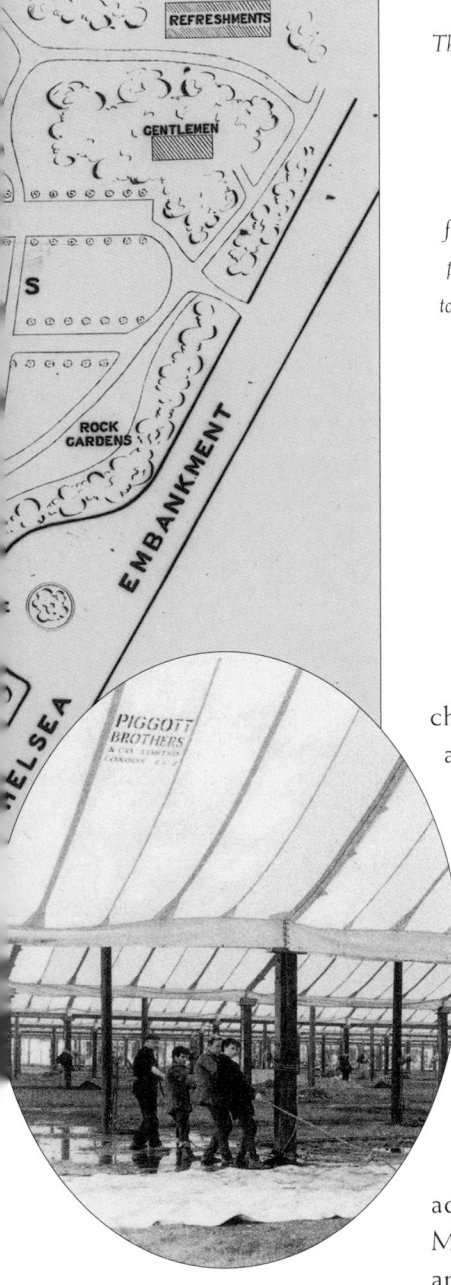

The Floral Pavilions, made of interchangeable PVC units, were introduced at the Chelsea Flower Show in 2000. Their great flexibility was expected to prove a considerable boon to organizers, visitors, and exhibitors alike.

MANY HANDS

The Essex firm of Piggotts Bros made successive canvas marquees for the Chelsea Flower Show, and each year they provided a team of up to 20 men to put them up.

challenging problem of enclosing once again the Chillianwallah monument. This was raised in memory of the officers and men of The Royal Welch Fusiliers who, under Lord Gough, fought a considerably greater force of Sikhs at Chillianwallah in 1849. The British army, technically, won this fiercely contested battle. Under the Great Marquee, the monument was more familiar to Chelsea visitors when wreathed in climbers or flowers.

The new structure has yet another advantage. Unlike the old, unwieldy Marquee, which was owned by the Society and stored by Piggotts, the new Pavilion is owned by a hiring company. The RHS rents the whole for the Chelsea Flower Show, but during the rest of the year any number of modules can be hired out for events that do not need the biggest marquee in the world. The Great Chelsea Pavilion doesn't

necessarily save the RHS any money, because the accumulative annual hiring costs exceeds that of purchasing new marquees every decade or so, but visitors are considerably safer and more comfortable.

The RHS then had to dispose of 13.6 acres (5.6 hectares) of elderly, off-white canvas duck: that is, 6.8 acres (2.8 hectares) – a large-sized field – of the old tent along with another 6.8 acres (2.8 hectares) from a previous cast-off, which was still stored in Ongar. The Old Chelsea Marquee Company was set up to sell a range of souvenir goods, which included gardening aprons, hats, bodywarmers and carrier bags for tools, made from the canvas of the Great Marquee. These were first sold with great success at Chelsea 2000 – and continued to be available for many years after. Many of Chelsea's firm friends love the idea of a bit of the show's tradition tied around their tummies.

JUDGEMENT DAYS

WINNING GOLD

In the early hours before the show first opens, the RHS Shows Department staff pin or balance the certificates against the display of each award winner. Here however the Evening Standard's Gold Medal award has subsequently been moved against a bottle of celebratory champagne.

"WINNING A MEDAL at Chelsea is the equivalent of getting to Oxbridge," explained Shows Director Stephen Bennett, putting the awards in their true perspective. "Those who receive a Gold, year after year, never lose the thrill of being on top of the world."

Theoretically Chelsea is just one of about 20 shows in the RHS annual calendar, each of which is judged in exactly the same way. Yet this is a little simplistic, because Chelsea is the most exciting flower show in the world, so everyone – exhibitors, judges, and visitors alike – scrutinizes the results with a quite different passion. Indeed it is a Chelsea tradition to criticize the judges' decisions, although they are used to that. "With so much at stake," said John Sales, Chairman of the Show Garden Assessors at Chelsea, "not least with garden sponsors wanting value for their often-considerable amounts of money, it is not surprising that the judging is anticipated with some excitement and the final verdict greeted with a degree of emotion … any implied criticism is bound to hurt. Especially with plants and gardens, opinions on merit are bound to vary and it is part of the game to rubbish the judges." As a result the RHS lays down very careful judging criteria to ensure fair play and to disarm the critics. These are clearly set out in the show's annual catalogue and exhibitors' manual.

Most awards at Chelsea are made to exhibits that are groups of different plants, flowers, fruit, or vegetables. An exhibit can be made up of one plant type alone, from roses to potatoes, in its many garden varieties, or might comprise different plant types, such as conifers or cacti. Alternatively the exhibit might concentrate on special growing techniques, such as bonsai. Other classes took in outdoor exhibits of plants in show and courtyard gardens, or those in display gardens inside the Pavilion. A further section is devoted to "plant material", the technical term for pieces of plant rather than whole plants: for example a floral arranger may make a picture of dried bark. Individual plants, too, can win awards, and then there are the education and scientific exhibits, which may or may not contain plants or plant material.

All medals, at Chelsea and in other shows, are awarded by the RHS Council via judging panels. A Gold Medal is the highest one, and it has no qualifications attached, nor is there any limit to the number awarded. If the judges decide you deserve a Gold, you will be given one.

Below this lofty level, the medals come in specific ranges. Show gardens, water and courtyard gardens, flowers, and ornamental plants qualify for Flora medals, in descending order of Silver-Gilt, Silver, or Bronze. Vegetable exhibits are awarded the same medals but in the Knightian range, while fruit (rarely shown) comes under the Hogg banner. The Lindley range of medals are awarded to scientific and educational exhibits, while Grenfell medals are for paintings, pictures, and photographs as well as floral arrangements and floristry.

(The distinction between floral arrangements and floristry is that the former are amateur flower clubs and the latter professional florists.)

If a grower has been exceptionally successful at cultivating a plant, an RHS Standing or Joint Committee can award a Certificate of Cultural Commendation without referring to the Council, while a Certificate of Appreciation might be handed to a display of educational or scientific horticultural interest. Judging panels also assess individual plants and may present a First Class Certificate (FCC), an Award of

Merit (AM), or a Certificate of Preliminary Commendation – in descending order of importance – to an individual plant of exhibition quality. Plants, too, may be singled out for further trials (not at Chelsea), where they may receive an Award of Garden Merit (AGM). Finally, if a plant is of exceptional botanic interest – a rare thing indeed today – it will be given a Botanical Certificate.

There is an enormous variation in the interest created by the awards. A Botanical Certificate may pass unnoticed by all but the most dedicated breeder, while the destiny of the Best Garden Award is often hugely controversial. "Any garden receiving a Gold Medal by a unanimous vote of the show garden panel can be considered for this award," explained Sales. Less contentious awards are trophies presented for the best window box, hanging basket, and floral arrangement, and for courtyard, garden design, and junior display (created by junior flower clubs), while Certificates of Merit are given to sundries stands with the strict rider that they are "awarded for excellence of presentation and not an RHS endorsement of the products or services on display."

THE JUDGES AND THEIR PANELS

In all about 450 people – some of them extremely grand horticulturists – make up the pool of voluntary members of RHS committees from which around 120 judges are selected for Chelsea. As

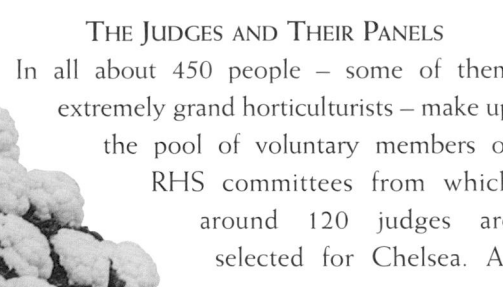

FINAL ADJUSTMENTS
The National Farmers' Union stand is given a last-minute check before the judges arrive. The magnificent cockerel weathervane, in this exhibit of 1995, was created with potatoes, carrots, beans, and parsley.

A MEETING OF MINDS
Judges congregate to assess the "Water Meadow Garden", designed by Mark Anthony Walker Landscape Architects in 1998. Impressed by its mature pollarded willows, reed beds, and water ditches, they awarded it a Gold Medal.

ROSA MOUNTBATTEN
('Harmantelle')
Rose of the Year 1982
Exhibited by Harkness Roses.

you might imagine, to be picked is an enormous honour, and every year the RHS brings in new judges to keep the process fresh and lively. About ten panels assess the floral exhibits in the various marquees with other panels for each remaining section, such as fruit, vegetables, educational exhibits, and show gardens. As well as this, the RHS also fields a panel of assessors – those with garden design experience – for both the show gardens and floristry exhibits.

"Each panel requires experience and balance, and must contain experts who have exhibited in the past. The annual Chelsea miracle of having flowers in May, which you normally see in January, June, or November, needs the experience of actually exhibiting to understand how difficult (or easy) this can be," commented Colin Ellis, the Council member responsible for judging. "We need enough eyes and minds to assess things fairly from all directions."

"There is no mystery about the judging process," Sales declared. "Including the marking schedule, the assessment criteria are available for anyone to see and are sent to all exhibitors. These criteria and the balance between them have been formulated over 20 years or so and are subject to annual review."

Obviously judges must look for high-quality, well-grown, and fresh-looking plants, which are carefully displayed and accurately labelled – but some other RHS criteria are more startling. The judges, for example, are told to ignore the source of the plants, so that an exhibitor who bought his plants from others has the same chance of success as one who has cultivated everything himself. The growers become pretty exercised about this. Yet, deconstructed, it is easy to see how the rule must stand. How can the judges know where each plant comes from? They can only be expected to judge what they see.

HOW THE JUDGING IS DONE

Judging of the show gardens takes place from 7.45am to 11am on the Monday (with security guards to keep everyone out of earshot in case these deliberations are overheard). The rest of the show is judged between 2.15pm and 5pm. (Exhibits in floristry, floral arrangements, junior displays, and garden design are replaced on Wednesday night, and the new exhibits

SWORD OF HONOUR

Up until the mid 1990s the champion among the winning show gardens used to be awarded 'The Sword of Honour'. In 1991 the Daily Express's "Forgotten Pavilion" won this important award.

NOSTALGIC MOOD

Show gardens frequently look back into the past. In 1988 Julian Dowle Partnership and Highfield Nurseries re-created the look of 1913 – the first Chelsea Flower Show – and won a Gold Medal.

assessed early on Thursday morning.)

Although the formal judging takes place on the Monday the whole process has actually begun over the preceding weekend. As most of the awards are made by the Council, its members individually spend time on Saturday, Sunday, and on the Monday morning looking at the 300 or so exhibits eligible for medals.

Meanwhile Ellis, along with the Director of Horticulture, Education, and Science, has toured the often-incomplete exhibits on the Saturday and Sunday before the show opens to assess if the judging panels contain the correct expertise to adjudicate on their allocated exhibits. If necessary two or more panels are asked to join together on the Monday to look at any exhibit where the combined expertise of more than one panel is required. "Fairness to every exhibitor is the keynote," explained Ellis.

"On the Sunday, also, a team of three or four assessors makes a detailed preliminary critique of each show garden, sometimes – unavoidably – before it is complete," said Sales. "These assessments, which include marks and comments against each of the criteria, are typed up in time for the judging the next morning. They are used as an aid to judging but do not dictate the outcome."

Judging on the Monday follows a well-tested routine: each panel meets at a set time, with its own chairman and secretary, to visit, examine, and discuss each exhibit. Because the show gardens are so theatrical – "to impress, to shock, to amuse, to evoke" – it is essential that the judges know what the designers' intentions are. "Great emphasis is therefore placed on the brief, written by each of the exhibitors to explain what they are trying to do, and for whom, and also to convey any assumpions made in relation to the site," Sales went on. "A well-written brief is the only solid basis for judging any flower-show garden. The award for each garden is decided at the site by a show of hands and the voting is recorded. At the end of the judging the range of awards is reviewed; borderline cases are reconsidered and revisited if necessary. All show awards are subject to ratification by the full Council." The panel chairman and secretary put the recommendations together and these are then co-ordinated by the Society's staff.

Confirmation of the awards is made by the RHS Council while the guests at the Gala Preview on the Monday evening drink

DELIGHTED DESIGNER

Rupert Golby flourishes his Gold Medal, which he won in 1997 for his "Centenary Garden".

Homeric amounts of champagne. The Council meets at 9pm for a session that goes on for three hours. "This all sounds like hard work, which it is, but it is also very worthwhile and enjoyable," commented Ellis. "The Council must take an overview of the whole show, enforce an overall standard, and be satisfied about the moderation of the judging. Most of the panels are chaired by Council members; yet one panel can be upbeat and another downbeat. It is important to emphasize that, although the Council has the exclusive right to award medals, it seeks not to change the recommendations of the panels, except when necessary to achieve fairness."

No one except the RHS Council and the administration is allowed to know the award winners until the Tuesday morning. The Council members therefore totter wearily to bed, while the Shows Department take over. Even though it is now very late, each medal card – about 300 in all – is neatly written out and delivered to the correct exhibit.

"We have generally finished distributing medal cards by dawn," said former Chelsea Show Exhibitor Manager Mavis Sweetingham. Now retired, she stayed up till 3am most Chelsea Monday nights. "Then I had two hours' sleep, a quick shower, and I was back again by 6am." The exhibitors start coming in and the show opens at 8am. Members can see whether they agree with the judges, and exhibitors are free to talk to the chairman of their judging panel about their displays.

CRITICAL ASSESSMENT

Judging window boxes and hanging baskets was meticulously carried out by a specialist panel, but pressure of space has resulted in these exhibits being moved to the Hampton Court Flower Show.

EATING AND ELGAR

WATER MUSIC

On Press Day a wide variety of performers are engaged to publicize the exhibits. Here, "Mole", "Ratty", and "Toad" play in Bunny Guinness's "Garden for Children" in 1994.

THE CHELSEA FLOWER SHOW is a traditional event and the organizers like to keep it that way. Ever since the first show, Chelsea visitors have drunk Pimm's by the gallon – a drink invented as far back as 1840 – and a band in Ranelagh Gardens has played the same Edwardian tunes to appreciative visitors. Such attractions have been encouraged by the organizers since it helps ease the congestion in the main part of the show.

Until 1995 the band had generally been that of the Grenadier Guards but they became too busy, so over the following three years the Household Division Band gradually assumed responsibility for music at Chelsea, although the Grenadiers' Jazz Quintet did play at the Gala Preview in 1999.

The Household Division Band fields various groups during the show. The main one thumps and tootles on the bandstand from 11am to 1pm and from 2.30pm to 4.30pm on Tuesday and Wednesday – the members' days. Some 25–28 musicians play three trombones, five trumpets, tuba, euphonium, flute, piccolo, oboe, six or seven clarinets, three saxophones (alto, tenor, and baritone), string bass, and percussion. For the 1999 Gala Preview night on the Monday, the Household Division provided a six-piece orchestra for a one-off dinner in aid of the Army Benevolent Fund, which was held in the Great Hall at the Royal Hospital.

Sam Lindley of the Household Division Band explained that their aim at Chelsea was to entertain: nothing too advanced, nothing too classical. "You can try to be clever but that's not what the public wants." To an extent, the music that current visitors hear is similar to what they would have heard in 1913. There are catchy tunes from the *Merry Widow* and the *Arcadians*, *Country Girl* and *Lilac Time* as well as airs from Gilbert and Sullivan and toe-tapping marches by Sousa. The 20th-century songs include the famous American musicals such as *Annie Get Your Gun* and *South Pacific* and the top ten tunes from Andrew Lloyd-Webber's shows.

"We have all served in Guards' bands," said Lindley, who plays

TRADITIONAL ENTERTAINERS

Music has always been an attraction for the general public. Since the very first Chelsea Flower Show, military bands (here the Grenadier Guards) have played popular and patriotic tunes to appreciative visitors.

OASIS OF CALM ▷
Ranelagh Gardens, offset from the bustle of the show, has always been a good place to relax while listening to the bandstand music.

trumpet and also acts as the band's impresario, "and there are a great many ex-Grenadiers among us. But it's hard for the Grenadiers themselves to get to Chelsea when they are so busy with Trooping of the Colour, Beating the Retreat, and the garden parties at Buckingham Palace … Chelsea is excellent for us because we can change into our uniforms at the Royal Hospital. We're all top-notch players and one of our clarinettists is ex-Covent Garden." When I ask him for his memories of a great disaster, Lindley is put out. "There are no cockups. The Guards know what to do." Even with his long-honed experience of playing at important events, Chelsea is something special. "It's like cricket at Lords – it has that special buzz."

A CHANGE OF RHYTHM

For many years, the NatWest Jazz Band played at the Gala Preview and then took its turn on the bandstand on the show days that are open to the general public: Thursday and Friday. The band actually had very little connection with the NatWest bank, although it was started among bank staff some 22 years ago and was originally called the NatWest Youth Band.

The band's spokesman was Stephen Davies. "We do lots of county shows – four days at the Royal Show, two at the Devon & Exeter, three at the Bath & West – but Chelsea is really prestigious for us. The Gala Preview is something entirely different – everyone is a celebrity. On public days there are three reasons why people come to listen

to us: they want to eat their sandwiches, their feet are exhausted, or sometimes they want to hear the music. It's nice to see the tapping feet. We play Dixieland jazz, *Alexander's Ragtime Band* and *Is it true what they say about … Chelsea*. We like to do things people know." The band fielded drums, banjo, sousaphone,

MUSICAL MOMENTS
To supplement the traditional music at Chelsea, the RHS sometimes introduces informal groups of musicians to entertain celebrities at the Gala Preview, on the Monday evening before the show opens.

trumpet, soprano saxophone, trombone, and a singer – John Moss, who also worked in the NatWest bank's Bishopgate branch. Sadly they disbanded in 2002, but thankfully the foot-tapping continued when Stephen Davis teamed up with Flexi Jazz's virtuoso Ged Horne to form the Chelsea Flower Show Jazz Band.

RECORD SALES

Ice-cream kiosks sell a lip-tingling 46,000 cups, cornets and bars in four days.

FOOD FOR THOUGHT

Just as the music is such an accepted part of Chelsea that the public rarely thinks about it, so is the catering. Visitors, swigging champagne or taking reviving draughts of tea on a hot afternoon, generally have no idea of the problems of feeding thousands of people in such a transient event.

Until 2003 the work was done by the catering firm of Gardner Merchant whose Town & County division had the sole catering contract for more than 15 years but they have recently been absorbed into the catering giant, Sodexho. Although they feed thousands of people at showgrounds

and seasonal events all over Britain, Chelsea is one of the most challenging tasks. Former Regional Director Russell Haddon explained that Gardner Merchant would plan for the following year while still working on the current year. "This enabled us to look at each area as it became operational and decide on any changes or improvements that might be needed."

"An event manager was given responsibility for each of our major events," Haddon went on. "He or she then discussed new ideas with the client. If the RHS was going to move or change an area, we could then plan accordingly. From the last day it became an ongoing process of planning. Accommodation would be reserved immediately after the event, some suppliers would also be booked, and the rest contacted during the year." The caterers then had regular meetings with the RHS to discuss how to plan the site and what services, such as power and water, are needed.

Some 800 guests a day are fed and watered in the corporate hospitality areas in Ranelagh Gardens, and no less than 40,000 people each day eat in the four main areas open to the public. There's a champagne and seafood restaurant, the Rock Bank Restaurant, which offers a variety of breakfasts, lunch and early evening meals, and other eating facilities. There are several Pimm's marquees open to the public, too. Private areas include the restaurant for the 400-odd

PICNIC FOR THREE

Despite the provision of more seats in the various restaurants, Pimm's bars, and food courts, some seasoned Chelsea-goers prefer to bring their own sustenance.

◁ **REFRESHING BREAK**
Visitors in 1987 here enjoy the warm sunny weather while having a lunchtime rest.

▽ **PRE-SHOW PAUSE**
Although there is a restaurant just for exhibitors once the show is officially open, they have to provide their own food during the build-up period.

exhibitors, who need a quiet break from the public, and the press tent, which is the centre for the media, especially on the Monday morning when 300 or more journalists, photographers, editors, and broadcasters turn up from all over the world. The RHS President has a marquee, which is used on the Monday to host the Royal Visit, and again later that day for two RHS receptions, after which it becomes a corporate hospitality tent. The RHS Council also has a private area where sponsors and exhibitors are feted and where the Council meets for its decision-making on show matters. There is a separate space for the RHS office staff, too, who of course also need vital refreshment.

DISASTERS STRIKE

EVERYONE BELIEVES THAT the Chelsea Flower Show has its own special atmosphere. There is plenty of jollity behind the scenes at this convivial event, and nowhere does this friendliness come out more than when there's a disaster brewing. This is the place to find the Dunkirk spirit alive some 60 years later.

Recently retired Chelsea Show Exhibitor Manager Mavis Sweetingham was, by definition, the RHS person in charge of disasters. She had the daunting task of anticipating and fending them off. For up to a year before each show was staged, she checked that the gardeners had sent in their designs and that every exhibitor could be fitted into the appropriate marquees.

Despite this ever-constant vigilance, Mavis Sweetingham has experienced plenty of disasters since her first days with the Society in 1977 (and she was Exhibitor Manager between 1987 and 2003). Most often disasters are caused by the weather. "During the build-up to the show I've seen torrential rain, snow, and scorching winds blowing off the River Thames, which, when the tide comes in, can be very, very cold. Olive trees need wrapping in fleece, and electric heaters have to be turned on. Then, just before the judges come round, we help whip off all the protective coverings."

In 1994, for example, the weather was icy. "Stapeley Water Gardens were showing Santa Cruz water lilies (*Victoria cruziana*),

READY FOR RAIN
At the end of May it can sometimes be wet and cold. Here, in 1923, visitors arrive at the showground dressed in warm coats and armed with large black umbrellas.

which like to sit in water of 80°F (26°C)," Mavis Sweetingham continued. "We were absolutely desperate. We put pumps into the pool, and on the top floated polystyrene borrowed from the Press tent. Then we brought hot water from the showers in plastic bins and tipped it in, yet we just couldn't keep the water warm enough. We know we're there to help exhibitors – and they all have problems at one time or another – but that was too great a challenge."

Tony Foxley, of Stapeley Water Gardens, also remembered that particular Chelsea very well. "It was a terrible May. We had to hire industrial heating kettles, the sort of thing used in army camps, with really large elements inside to try and keep the water warm, but it didn't really work. Everything

flopped, and the tropical plants died. It was a disaster – the worst Chelsea ever."

"At other times," Mavis Sweetingham commented, "we've had torrential rain washing into the marquee stands, and we've all been crawling under the canvas screens around the exhibitors' stands, trying to lift them off the floor. Even RHS Council members have assisted. The point about Chelsea is that, if there's a problem, every single person will turn out to help – the public never realizes that." It is just as well, perhaps, that visitors are unaware that those expert horticulturists who award the medals have earlier been scuffling under canvas screens, desperate to prevent a whole show flooding. On another occasion, the deluge was too much for Julie Toll's sunken garden, which seemed about to disappear under water. "We

MISERY DAY

On Members' Day 1971 the rain had been so heavy that wellington boots were required at the Chelsea Flower Show.

were pumping it out until just before the judging but, luckily, the weather lifted in time."

Sometimes, lack of water is a problem. One Members' day in the early 1990s, a digger punctured a water main in Chelsea Bridge Road, near the showground, in the middle of the morning. All water supplies at the show stopped at once. "I was in the Press tent at the time," remembered Shows Director Stephen Bennett. "Although some journalists asked how the gardens could be watered, my priority was the 40,000 people in the grounds. How would we manage without the toilets and, in the run-up to lunchtime, how could the caterers wash their hands?"

The Shows Department sprang into action. Thames Water was asked for help and immediately sent a fleet of water tankers. These had to park outside the Bull-Ring Gate, because it was too dangerous to allow them to

drive inside the crowded grounds. Water pipes and pumps were then manoeuvred into position throughout the show. Thames Water also repaired the break within four hours. "They were brilliant," Bennett recalled. Meanwhile the public had to be alerted to the fact that the toilets had no water, "which my old colleague Ruth Anders, who was known as 'The Voice' at Chelsea, did over the public-address system. The members reacted with good humour and a stiff upper lip." Bennett's next dilemma was what to do when the water came back on. "We couldn't tell everyone at once, so we said nothing – probably some people left early."

DISASTERS EN ROUTE TO CHELSEA

Sometimes accidents happen before exhibits even reach the show. Mavis Sweetingham remembered the embarrassed faces at Askham Bryan Agricultural College one year. "They were going to exhibit a Scottish-themed rock garden bank covered with heather, which some students were to drive down from Leeds. On their way, one student threw a cigarette butt out of the window and it fell on the heather, which caught alight. People on the motorway kept pointing at the van." The students, blithely believing that the car drivers were admiring their splendid display, drove on with the burning heather bank in flames behind them, until the fire really caught hold. All three emergency services turned out to douse the blaze (and rescue the students), by which time the college's whole display had burnt.

On yet another occasion Mavis Sweetingham recalled an exhibitor asking the RHS staff to watch his trailer as he drove through the narrow gates to the Chelsea showground. "But you haven't got a trailer,"

GARRYA ELLIPTICA
Award of Merit 1975
Exhibited by Lord Aberconway.

◁ **TROPICAL VISITOR**
Cold weather during the 1994 show destroyed an exhibit of Santa Cruz water lilies (Victoria cruziana), which come from tropical South America and could not be kept warm enough. Their unusual, 6ft (2m) wide leaves turn up sharply at the edges – like giant tea trays.

they told him, puzzled. He had not — it had become uncoupled on his journey to London and been left behind on the fast lane of the M4. All his plants were still in it.

One of the howlers that many staff remember occurred in the mid 1990s. "An exhibitor had designed a really over-the-top conservatory with a Romeo and Juliet theme. They had ordered an enormous 40ft [12m] palm tree from Italy. When the driver turned up at the Bull-Ring Gate, he found he just could not get his lorry in, so he parked it there and just went off." The famed Chelsea can-do spirit took over where the Italian driver had left off. "We had tree movers on site for the gardens and they worked for three nights to get it into the right place. Then when we off-loaded it, we found that the tree couldn't be stabilized so we had to tie it up to an oak tree in the Royal Hospital grounds.

"Every show has its own problems. On one occasion the Belgian stand collapsed just a few minutes after the Queen came round. The exhibitors took away all the debris and by the following morning, when the show officially opened, you would never have known it had happened," Mavis Sweetingham went on. "Another time, on the South African stand, a column covered with proteas and other plants was pulled over just before the Royal Visit. It smashed the stand, yet, with that super atmosphere, everyone rallied around and the stand was successfully rebuilt."

"One year when it was pouring with rain," remembered Jekka McVicar, who has consistently won Gold Medals for her herbal displays, "there was Mavis Sweetingham, completely dressed in yellow fishermen's oilskins, conducting the traffic. That's the spirit of Chelsea — that's the team."

DANGEROUS SPIKES
Umbrellas at Chelsea are a source of two potential disasters: they can be lost, or else they might poke someone in the face, especially in a particularly crowded situation such as here, in Main Avenue during the 1993 show.

GLORIOUS GARDENS

> " *The organizers try to inject as much variety of theme, style, planting, and structure as possible into the show.* "

COUNTRY COTTAGE
This "New England Cottage Garden" won a Gold Medal for its designer Fiona Lawrenson, in 1996.

THE SHOW GARDENS at Chelsea today are among the most marvellous in the world. They take a year or more to conceive and up to £200,000 to execute. (Rumours that the most expensive cost £1 million are probably untrue, but every sponsor is very coy about costs.)

The detail involved in a show garden is fantastic. A rectory garden in 1995 required daisies to be dug into its pristine lawns, and a show garden in 1997 included pavilions built with old bricks and furnished with bees-waxed antiques. In 1999, assistants could be seen vacuuming or otherwise titivating crystal-clear sheets of water and rills for fear that the odd leaf or bud-casing had fallen in. Other show gardens contain sizeable trees or sturdy-looking buildings. The centrepiece of "Sally Clarke's Kitchen Garden" of 1996 was an ancient, interestingly gnarled olive tree transplanted from Italy, and the "Old Abbey Garden", sponsored by the *Daily Telegraph* in 1994, was decorated with Gothic stonework, including a parapet from Salisbury Cathedral, which had been replaced during conservation work. The 1999 "Garden of the Book of Gold", which was sponsored by His Highness Shaikh Zayed bin Sultan Al-Nahyan, featured 12 date palms (*Phoenix dactylifera*), 40ft (12m) tall, set around a rectangular pool of water. Such exotic trees had to be flown in specially from the Arabian desert.

The open-air sites are in huge demand from garden designers. Every March, 14 months before the show opens, all designers who have asked are sent an invitation to apply for a show garden, by the RHS. About 50 applications are returned every

◁ "GARDEN OF THE BOOK OF GOLD", *Charles Funke Associates, 1999.*

year and these are eventually whittled down to around 25 actual gardens – the number depending on the sizes of the sites.

One of the most important criteria in selecting a particular designer is whether he or she has found any sponsorship, according to former Chelsea Show Exhibitor Manager Mavis Sweetingham. "Occasionally a sponsor can fall through, leaving a gap." In January 1999 she was planning on 25 actual gardens for the show that year, but two were still waiting for a firm sponsor. "It was leaving it very, very late, and until we get confirmation nothing can be definite." In the end, only 22 gardens made it to the hallowed turf of Chelsea 1999.

PRIMULA
PRESENTATION
The charming 18th-century idea of creating a theatre for showy auriculas is a welcome appearance at the show.

The organizers try to inject as much variety of theme, style, planting, and structure as possible into the show, but zeitgeist often defeats them: white gardens, country houses, and classical statues will be fashionable one year, while applications another year will focus on sweet little cottage gardens, railway sidings, and sheds in the outback of Australia.

"One year we had two Japanese gardens," recalled Mavis Sweetingham. "We put them adjacent to each other: they were such a contrast that we thought it would help people understand Japanese design. One was minimalist with very few plants but stones and paving, while the second was less formal and had much more bamboo."

DIFFERENCES IN QUALITY
The standard of entry also varies. "Some years are strong: 1999 was rather mixed. I don't know why," Mavis Sweetingham continued. In 1999 some

PUBLICITY FOR A PAPER
In 1994 the Daily Telegraph *sponsored this "Old Abbey Garden", which included old architectural stonework from Salisbury Cathedral. The paper has been a regular sponsor of show gardens.*

A Cool Classic

This "Classical Garden" of 1994 revived another 18th-century style — that of French parterres and pleached limes — along with a tunnel arbour planted with roses. Harpers & Queen *and* Cartier *provided the financial backing for this Michael Miller creation.*

Contemporary Style

Dan Pearson's modern design for the Evening Standard *in the 1994 Chelsea Flower Show was entitled "A Vibrant London Garden". To make it more realistic, the garden included "found urban objects".*

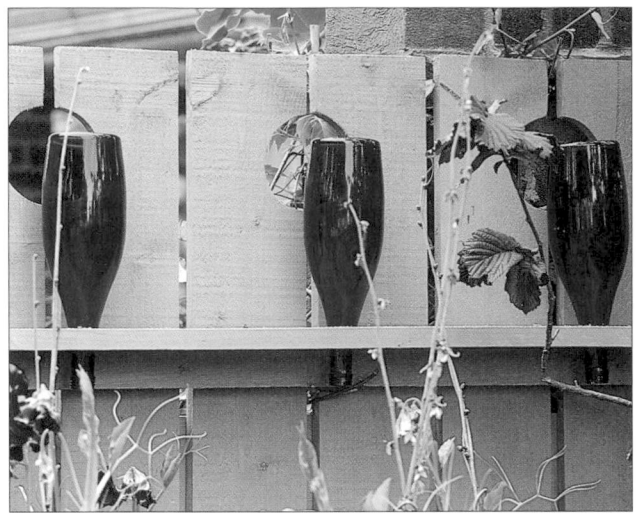

traditionalist visitors predictably derided Sir Terence Conran's "Chef's Roof Garden" as not having sufficiently interesting plants, while a few modernist ones were unimpressed by Michael Balston's traditionally planted "*Daily Telegraph* Reflective Garden", even though it received the Best Garden Award and, of course, a Gold Medal.

In June, 11 months before every show, each designer has to submit a sketch of his or her show garden, along with a preliminary planting plan, an axonometric projection, and details of the contractual and sponsorship arrangements. By the end of July these pass for provisional selection to the Society's Chelsea Gardens Committee and, by late September, each designer must send in every detail of his plan, along with a list of plants. "The real reason we ask for a complete plant list is that we want to confirm that the plants will be available and in peak condition," explained Mavis Sweetingham. "May is a difficult time, with only rhododendrons and azaleas flowering at their correct season. The

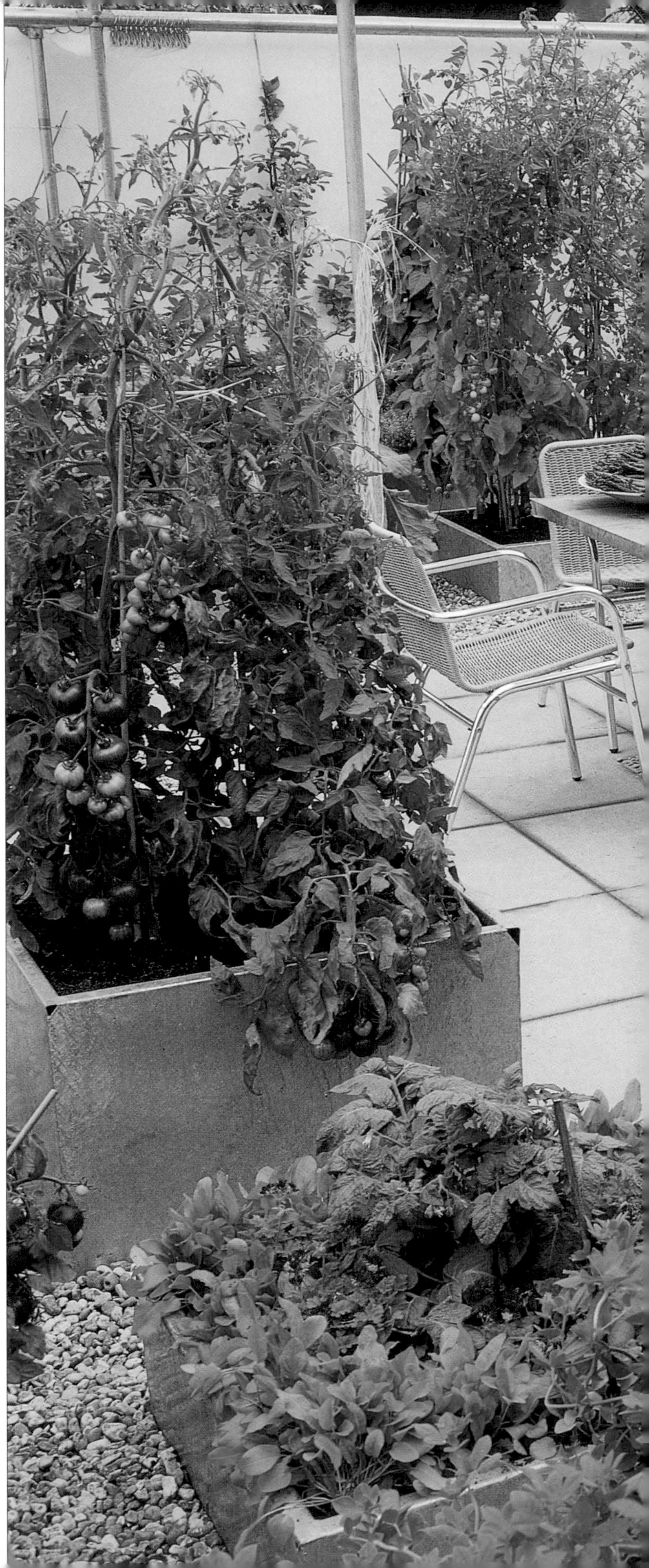

BEDTIME MUSINGS

White canvas curtains surrounded Sir Terence Conran's Gold Medal-winning "Chef's Roof Garden" of 1999 for the Evening Standard and Laurent Perrier. Reputedly Sir Terence thought up the idea of such screens while lounging in bed.

EDIBLE PLANTS

Conran's winning garden was notable for its imaginative use of vegetables, such as 'Redbor' purple kale, all of which might be grown on a roof garden or terrace.

PARADISE REGAINED

Sponsored by the Daily Telegraph *and American Express in 1998, Sarah Raven designed a "Primitive Garden" – a lush and voluptuous Eden, full of brilliant colours, textures, and scents.*

ROSA 'AMERICAN PILLAR'

This rambling rose made its first appearance at Chelsea only in 194? even though it was first produced b Van Fleet in 1902.

SPANISH INFLUENCE
Until the 1960s most show gardens at Chelsea had a British theme – this Spanish garden being erected for the 1939 show would have been an exception.

rest of the plants must be forced or held back." The Society also wants to be certain that the garden and its designer are worthy: if the central element of a Chelsea Flower Show was to be distinctly dowdy, the show would quickly lose its cachet. And, as Chelsea charges no entry fee for a show garden, its demands are quite justifiable.

RHS scrutiny can, however, fall down on occasions. Paul Cooper's 1994 "A Constructivist Garden" was based on heavy-breathing allusions to sex. The design was an outdoor bedroom with plants ("flowers are the sexual organs of plants") decked in jewellery and used teabags. RHS staff had to remove homoerotic pictures, for fear they would offend the Queen, and the Society stated that the designer had not revealed his true intentions in his original application. "The RHS takes a dim view of this sort of thing at Chelsea," sniffed Shows Director Stephen Bennett, at the time.

A FASHION FOR ROCK GARDENS

The importance of garden designers is fairly recent at Chelsea. In early shows, when all gardens were either formal ones or rock gardens, emulating the Alps or a wild Highland scree, the nurserymen planned, designed, planted, and constructed their own show gardens. There are old pictures of men in flat caps and trousers tied below the knee labouring away to create outcrops of slate while the head gardener, in a bowler hat, directs them from firm ground. The 1913 show included 17 rock or formal gardens, while, in 1916, the *Gardeners' Chronicle* noted dourly, "only one show garden – much the same as last year". By 1919 there were "fewer [show] gardens than before but several rock gardens". In 1920 there was topiary "for the first time for several years ... tastes may differ as to their value in the garden".

In 1922 the rock gardens "were not as good as usual, the boulders were too sparse and unkempt", complained the *Gardeners' Chronicle*. They looked more like "hill tops around some of our southern seaside resorts than Alpine scenery". The anonymous gardening critic of the *Gardeners' Chronicle* was an inveterate grumbler: in 1924 he found the rock gardens "scarcely so pleasing or effective" as before, and in 1925 John Klinkert's topiary and yew "sombre and formal".

In 1929, Mrs Sherman Hoyt introduced the first real show garden in what is now the modern style

START OF AN ERA
John Brookes's sparse and modernist garden of 1962 was one of the first show gardens to be created by a garden designer rather than a nurseryman.

and it astounded Chelsea visitors, with its theatrical style and use of inventive props. The garden was an inspired piece of theatre that was half a century before its time, and it won a Gold Medal. Sherman Hoyt's mission was to attract worldwide attention to the plants of her native state (California), so she brought over three gardens from there. The *Gardeners' Chronicle* reported, "She loves the desert plants of California and desires to show them in as natural conditions as possible. To people who cannot see the desert, she brings the desert to them."

Sherman Hoyt's gardens represented Death Valley, a Desert Garden, and Redwood Grove. Death Valley had salt craters, lime stalactites, cacti, and the essential skeleton of a

LORD A LEAPING
An important indication that garden design was in fact an acceptable profession came when Lord Snowdon designed an aviary for Waterer's show garden in 1970.

burro. The Desert Garden, inspired by the Mojave and Colorado deserts, contained a small rock pool beside which was a battered board marked "Poison Water Beware" and a skull-and-crossbones to emphasize the point. Plants included a parched *Yucca arborescens* (now known as *Y. brevifolia*), prickly pears, scrubby creosote bushes, cacti, and smoke trees. The Redwood Grove was enchanting. Sherman Hoyt did not bring in giant redwoods but settled for an impression of its forest floor, with ferns such as *Polystichum munitum*, *Woodwardia radicans*, and *Polypodium californicum* along with seedling Douglas firs (*Pseudotsuga menziesii*).

RISE OF THE PROFESSIONAL DESIGNER
Only in 1962 were there real signs that professional garden designers, as opposed to plantsmen, were becoming dominant. This was the year John Brookes arrived at Chelsea. He was trained as an architect, rather than a horticulturist, and his garden was clearly influenced by this. As winner of an architect's garden competition, he created a Chelsea show garden for the Institute of Landscape. He was possibly the first designer to take on a show garden – hitherto they had been the preserve of growers and nurserymen. Another interesting garden that year was a plan for soldiers' married quarters, sponsored by the War Office.

By 1998 show garden design had reached a peak of fashion when Karl Lagerfeld of Chanel was heavily photographed in "Le Bosquet de Chanel", his evocation of the style of garden Madame Chanel would have planted.

It was some time before the change to professional designers became apparent. Three years after John Brookes' appearance, the Institute of Landscape again tried to bring design to the forefront, with a garden designed by K.A. Neivens. This had a municipal theme and concrete bowl fountains. "This type of garden will not appeal to everyone," noted the *Gardeners' Chronicle* with characteristic firmness.

Another real boost to garden designers came in 1970 when Lord Snowdon designed a Gothic aviary for the Waterer's garden; the aviary was made by film-set makers at the Elstree Studios, when work was short, at the request of the film director Bryan Forbes. The garden won a Gold Medal for its designer Graham Thomas and, more significantly, implied that garden design was now a respectable occupation. This set a trend that led to the glamorous shows of today.

In 1972 the *Financial Times*, which had sponsored a garden in 1971, first asked the designer John Brookes to create a waterside garden, and in 1975 the Inchbald School of Design received a Gold Medal for their "Moonlit Garden". Finally in 1979 "exhibitors have begun to realize the value of an outdoor garden", according to designers Faith and Geoff Whiten in their book, *The Chelsea Flower Show*, after the public had flocked to see the smartest creations.

The peak in designer chic came 20 years later, in 1998, when fashion designer Karl Lagerfeld, the house of Chanel's designer, created a show garden for his employer, which he called "Le Bosquet de Chanel". In 1999 the only fashion designer at Chelsea was Bruce Oldfield, who helped on the *Express*'s "Horti-Couture" garden. To balance the lack of heavyweight fashion designers that year, there was

Sir Terence Conran, the multi-faceted designer par excellence, with his "Chef's Roof Garden". This combined hard design and gardening with his other great interest, restaurants. One television gardener – Carol Klein – made a garden, entitled "21st Century Street", in 1999, but then she was a professional gardener before she became a television personality. It can't be long, however, before television takes over the Chelsea show gardens, as it seems to be taking over gardening elsewhere.

DESIGNS AND DESIGNERS

IMMEDIATELY THE SHOW opened for the first Press Day of the Millennium, it was clear that Chelsea 2000 would be far more important than just for the novelty of the new Floral Pavilions. The standard of the show gardens was exceptional but, even more important, it was obvious that they would be an important influence on gardening and garden design for the foreseeable future.

Perhaps the most inspiring of these gardens, certainly with hindsight, was the combined work of Arne Maynard and Piet Oudolf who together created "Evolution" for *Gardens Illustrated*. In one smallish plot, they brought together the notion of cloud hedges, Persian carpet planting (an idea also used by the Prince of Wales in 2001 when Michael Miller used an old rug from Highgrove for "The Carpet Garden") and the surprise element of a water feature powered by new technology. H≈WOW created jumping jets of water which sprang from one stainless steel bowl to the next – a neat twist on 17th century surprise fountains. Less surprisingly, it won best garden as well as a gold.

The complex mixture of formality and prairie type planting was also evident in Tom Stuart-Smith's "Homage to Le Nôtre" and formality and water came together for

INSPIRATIONAL PLANTING
"Evolution" won Best Garden in the important 2000 show for designers Piet Oudolf and Arne Maynard and Gardens Illustrated *magazine. It proved to be one of the most influential gardens for several years.*

Arabella Lennox-Boyd's "A Garden for All Time". But the garden which I found most inspiring was Ryl Nowell's evocation of the vegetable garden at the Chateau de Bosmelet in Normandy. Her "Gardens sans Frontières" proved to those who have forgotten it that vegetables are colourful and decorative too.

Sadly, after the millennium blast, the gardens of the following shows were often disappointing. There has been a constant need for gimmickry – painted cones and tyre-like objects, water features that, unlike those in 2000, were neither beautiful nor relevant, hard landscaping instead of plants. Where once every Chelsea would produce at least two gardens of tasteful white Sackville-West planting and old rectories, those from 2000 on have generally preferred

CLASSY CONTRAST
Tom Stuart-Smith won best garden in 2003 for Laurent-Perrier and Harpers & Queen *with this elegantly cool planting of perennials and grasses under* Cornus kousa *trees. The designer is known for his consistent, evolving style.*

A CAMEO OF YORKSHIRE COUNTRYSIDE
Julian Dowle's celebration of Yorkshire in 2003 was very popular with show visitors, especially as it featured a typically Yorkshire dry stone wall and an evocative mix of cottage garden and native plants.

the instant makeover look.

Some designers, however, continue to evolve their own styles. Tom Stuart-Smith, whose garden for Laurent Perrier and Harpers & Queen won Best in Show in 2003, created waving, colourful prairie planting under multi-trunked *Cornus kousa;* Christopher Bradley-Hole took over from Charles Funke Associates to

GRAND GARDENER
The 1993 Country Living/Kelways *garden "A Celebration of Gertrude Jekyll featured a lookalike of the grande dame. Jane Fearnley-Whittingstall's design highlighted Jekyll's trademerk cottage planting.*

design a desert garden for His Highness Shaikh Zayed Bin Sultan Al-Nahyan retaining his ingenious planting and abstract elegance the while and Peter Tinsley was as always a master of rock formations, his 2003 "Visions of Snowdon" being even more rugged than 2000's "Cumbria in Bloom". HM Prison, Leyhill which had regularly produced worthy but dull show gardens at Chelsea, suddenly burst into life in 2000 with a gold medal winning, and very popular, "Time the Healer" followed in 2003 with "No Time to Stand and Stare". Both were in another burgeoning genre: the semi-wild, overgrown garden with essential collapsing hut.

CHANGING FASHIONS

Although the organizers of Chelsea do try very hard to vary the styles of the show gardens at each event and from year to year, circumstances may well defeat them, such is the zeitgeist in the air. Garden design is increasingly swayed by fashion, television's rapid response and the needs of designers constantly to innovate. In the early years of the show, and up until the involvement of designers rather than horticulturists in the 1960s, garden fashion was almost static. While Peter Tinsley is virtually the only rock garden designer to show today, at one point there were dozens.

In the 1980s and early 1990s, from copying romantic nature in the wild, the mood veered to embrace country-house style – a look inspired by the great duo of English lady gardeners, Gertrude Jekyll and Vita Sackville-West. White gardens, red gardens, challenging vistas and belvederes, old-fashioned roses and brilliant but very labour-intensive herbaceous borders were

AN IDEAL FUTURE
*In her "21st Century Street"
design for Channel 4 in
1999, Carol Klein created
an organic and self-
sustaining world in which
waste was recycled, water
conserved, and plants could
be readily propagated.*

◁ REVIVED GLORIES
For "Mr Maidment's Garden" in 1994, which was sponsored by You magazine and Yardley, Stephen Woodhams removed an ancient Victorian greenhouse from a garden in Dorset and reconstructed it at Chelsea. The showpiece exemplified the new fashion for evoking crumbling, run-down gardens on large country estates.

REFLECTING GARDEN HISTORY ▷
A "Garden in Homage to Le Notre" was Tom Stuart-Smith's entry for Chelsea 2000 for the Garden History Society with Historic Royal Palaces. The mixture of formal, symmetrical topiary with colourful, perennial beds is entirely consistent with his subtle style.

reproduced wholesale from the manor houses of England. This charming but overworked style was evoked by Isabel and Julian Bannerman in their "Old Abbey Garden" for *The Daily Telegraph* in 1994 – a far cry from the aptly-named "Wrong Garden" designed by James Dyson and Jim Honey for the newspaper in 2003 – and, the following year, by Arabella Lennox-Boyd in her centenary garden for the National Trust.

PROFESSIONAL VISITOR
Roddy Llewelyn, whose show garden in the late 1980s won a Silver-Gilt Medal, is a regular visitor to Chelsea.

In 1996, *Harpers & Queen*, teamed with Cartier rather than Laurent Perrier, produced a homage to Vita Sackville-West and they, at least, have never wavered from the elegant. In 1997, *Country Life* celebrated its own centenary with a garden as stately as the houses it advertises, designed by Rupert Golby and featuring two old brick pavilions inspired by Major Lawrence Johnston's Hidcote. Then, in 1998 Michael Miller designed a garden, again for *Harpers & Queen* and Cartier, inspired by the Prince of Wales's garden at Highgrove. (The association between the Prince and Miller was repeated

ROCK REVIVAL

At early Chelsea Flower Shows rock and water gardens were extremely popular, but their numbers have declined since the 1960s, when the new breed of professional designer arrived at the show. In 1999 Peter Tinsley bucked this trend with his "Garden from the Valleys of Wales".

**YUCCA GLORIOSA
'VARIEGATA'**
*Award of Merit 1982
Exhibited by Notcutts of Woodbridge.*

in 2001.) Despite its organic elements and fashionable wild-flower meadows designed by Miriam Rothschild, the expert in the field, this show garden was still heavily influenced by Jekyll and Sackville-West.

Jekyll would have been as much at home with the continuing theme of cottage gardens, which have appeared every single year I've visited the show variously adorned with rusting watering cans, old motor cars, bicycles and tractors and ebullient nettles. Jekyll adored the vernacular both in planting and architecture so she took as much an interest in English cottage gardens as those of manor houses. Her influence can be seen in 1994's "Mr Maidment's Garden" by Stephen Woodhams, who combined the country house garden with the cottage garden by taking a genuinely dilapidated corner from a grand house in Dorset. It had a broken-down Victorian greenhouse, stagnant water, nettles and other weeds – shabby chic had arrived in the garden. More rural still were "A Cottage Garden at Railway Cuttings" in the same year, 1996's "New England Cottage Garden", the "Quarry Man's Garden" in 1998, "Mr McGregor's Garden" of 1999. Even the millennium was not immune, with HM Prison Leyhill's "Time the Healer" (featuring a tree stump and shed) and, in, 2001, Paul Stone's "Lifetime Care Garden" for Help the Aged (complete with honeysuckle and washing lines.)

CHARITY AND EDUCATION

Another theme which runs through the modern Chelsea gardens is of charities and pressure groups using the show's clout to shout a message. This may be as simple as the National Asthma Campaign's efforts to encourage the planting of flowers with low

pollen counts or as complex as Flora for Fauna's ecological efforts. In 1998 George Carter made "The Bird's Buffet" using native English plants to feed the birds and insects. Worries of conservationists and the reality of global warming (though Chelsea 2003 was held in intermittent drizzles and downpours, unlike the following months' heatwaves) have led to water being a constant feature over the last 10 years. Water tumbles over slate, arches from fountains, lies serene in rills and dribbles downwards, or in the Wrong Garden's case, seemingly upwards in streams. Keeping the variety going, along with

MEDITERRANEAN GARDEN
*Christopher Bradley-Hole's "Latin Garden",
sponsored by the Daily Telegraph and
American Express, used traditional and
high-tech materials, and took its inspiration
from the pastoral tradition of Virgil. It won
the Best Garden Award in 1997.*

FOR HEALTH AND BEAUTY

Purporting to belong to an amateur herbalist, designer Bunny Guinness planted culinary, cosmetic, and medicinal plants, including aspirin-creating willows, in this "Herbalist's Garden". It was sponsored by Wyevale Garden Centres in 1998.

cottage gardens and country house borders, designers were at last making modernism convincing. These were urban gardens for the young and chic. Dan Pearson created "A Vibrant London Garden" in 1994 and, two years later, his influential "London Roof Garden" for the 1990s, suitably enough for the *Evening Standard*. Drifts of grasses and scented herbs inspired a new way of planting perennials and foreshadowed Oudolf and Maynard's work in 2000. Even more convincing to me was Christopher Bradley-Hole's "Latin Garden" (sponsored by the *Daily Telegraph*) which won the Best Garden award in 1997. I don't think his controlled planting of irises and alliums alongside concrete and water has yet been equalled.

In 1999 Sir Terence Conran was using vegetables (though not so whole-heartedly as Ryl Nowell's "Gardens sans Frontiers") in his gold-medal winning "Chef's Roof Garden". He demonstrated his mastery of current fashion even if the horticulturists tutted that it was a triumph of design over gardening. That, in itself, was and is highly influential. Sponsored again by the *Evening Standard* along with Laurent Perrier, the garden also boasted galvanised-iron planters (now a cliché) filled with such combinations as Tuscan cavolo nero and purple chives which, together, would make a tasty dish.

A CHANGE IN EMPHASIS

Just as fashions in food and clothes have been moving towards fusion – sushi with salsa, mandarin jackets with Manolos – so have gardens. Japanese gardeners have made the effort to cross the world to design at Chelsea for 2001's "Real Japanese Garden" (*Daily Telegraph*) the "Tateshima Meadow" of 2002 and, in 2003 Kay Yamada did a Japanese take on the English garden. The "Abu Dhabi" influence is constant and, in 2003, Bonterra Vineyards arrived with Californian wildflowers, organic vines and a cork oak tree, following American Beth Miller's attempt in 2002 to get people to take water shortages seriously.

REVOLUTIONARY

Where will the show gardens of Chelsea go next? Has minimalism peaked; is bedding-out set for a revival (as at Waddesdon); are grasses already a cliché? Curiously, we still need to look at the ideas of that octogenarian revolutionary, Christopher Lloyd, whose gardens at Great Dixter (and not at Chelsea where he has never exhibited) are always overturning received wisdom and garden snobbery.

COUTURE AND FLOWERS

For his "Horti-Couture" garden in 1999 (right), garden designer James Alexander-Sinclair joined forces with fashion designer Bruce Oldfield. They mixed plants with fashion – and models (below) – to imply that by the end of the 20th century gardening was really chic. A special attraction was a water jet, which cut itself off in mid-air.

CHANEL'S CREATION

THE PEAK IN DESIGNER garden chic arrived in 1998, when Karl Lagerfeld, Chanel's dark-glassed and pony-tailed designer and a man with a passion for 18th-century gardens, descended (by private jet, of course) on Chelsea, with the editors of American, British, and French *Vogue* in tow. He was also accompanied by a clutch of supermodels, who were bemused by the gardening press – some of whom had never heard of them. Lagerfeld came to see the garden that he had helped design between collections of haute couture. "Coco Chanel was French, so I made a French garden," he told the *Sunday Telegraph*. "And she loved the 18th century, so I made a bosquet." A bosquet, he explained, "was a kind of room in a wood where ladies could sit ... Madame Chanel loved camellias, so we had to have camellias in this garden, and everything in white." Then he added, "I love gardening, only I don't like getting my hands dirty."

▽ SETTING UP
Careful preparation for this complex design meant that time taken to assemble it at the show was kept to a minimum. Several dress rehearsals had been held before the materials were transported to Chelsea.

◁ PREPARING THE BOX PARTERRE
Months before the show, box bushes were planted in wire containers under polythene, in the exact patterns of the planned knot garden. Each container measured 2 x 1ft (60 x 30cm) and was numbered for quick positioning when it reached the showground. The containers were hidden by topsoil and immaculately raked gravel.

◁ GOLDEN GIRL
The focal point of "Le Bosquet de Chanel" of 1998, on which Tom Stuart-Smith did much of the basic design, was a copy of the famous Venus de Medici. The nude was entirely covered in 22-carat gold, which glittered against a dark green background. The screen of container-grown hornbeams was forced into growth in the greenhouses behind.

△ PEDESTAL PRECINCT
Plywood was carefully measured to create staging for the Chanel garden, and this was then concealed under flagstones and gravel.

TOP PRIZE ▷
This Gold Medal-winning design was rumoured to be the most expensive show garden ever created: amounts such as £1 million were firmly denied by the fashion firm.

GAINING A GOLD

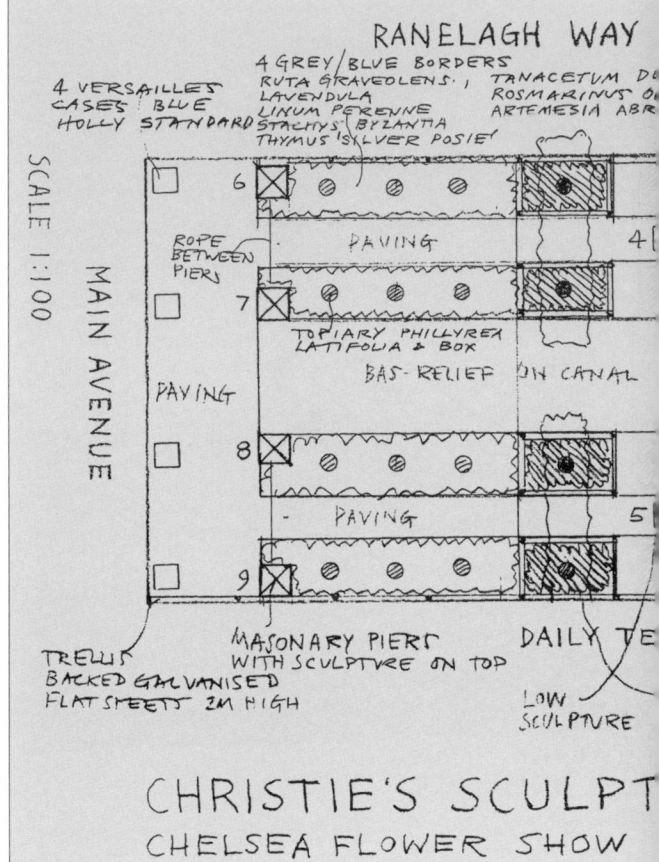

CHRISTIE'S FINE ART AUCTIONEERS, as sponsor, and George Carter, as designer, were perfect partners for a Chelsea show garden. Christie's have been steeped in the art world since 1766, selling everything from Botticelli pictures and Beatles' guitars to garden statues and the contents of 18th-century English country houses and Italian palaces. George Carter, who is fascinated by garden history, is a trained sculptor and landscape designer, and has designed high-profile sales such as that of Princess Diana's dresses for Christie's, as well as exhibitions at the

MATCHING SET
George Carter designed four classically inspired gilded sculptures – representing sun, rain, frost, and lightning – to top the four soft grey pillars at the front of his 1999 show garden, which was entitled "Sculpture in the Garden".

Queen's Gallery at Buckingham Palace and at her gardens in Windsor Great Park.

In 1998 Christie's had at the last moment sponsored a garden designed by Carter for the charity Flora for Fauna. "We were a bit of a white knight," admitted Christie's Head of Marketing Meredith Etherington-Smith. "Carter had done our windows at King Street, St James's in London, and designed special installations for our important sales such as those for Nureyev and Diana and has a history of working for us. The 1999 garden, which coincided with his other life as a landscape designer, was our first proper collaboration with him at Chelsea."

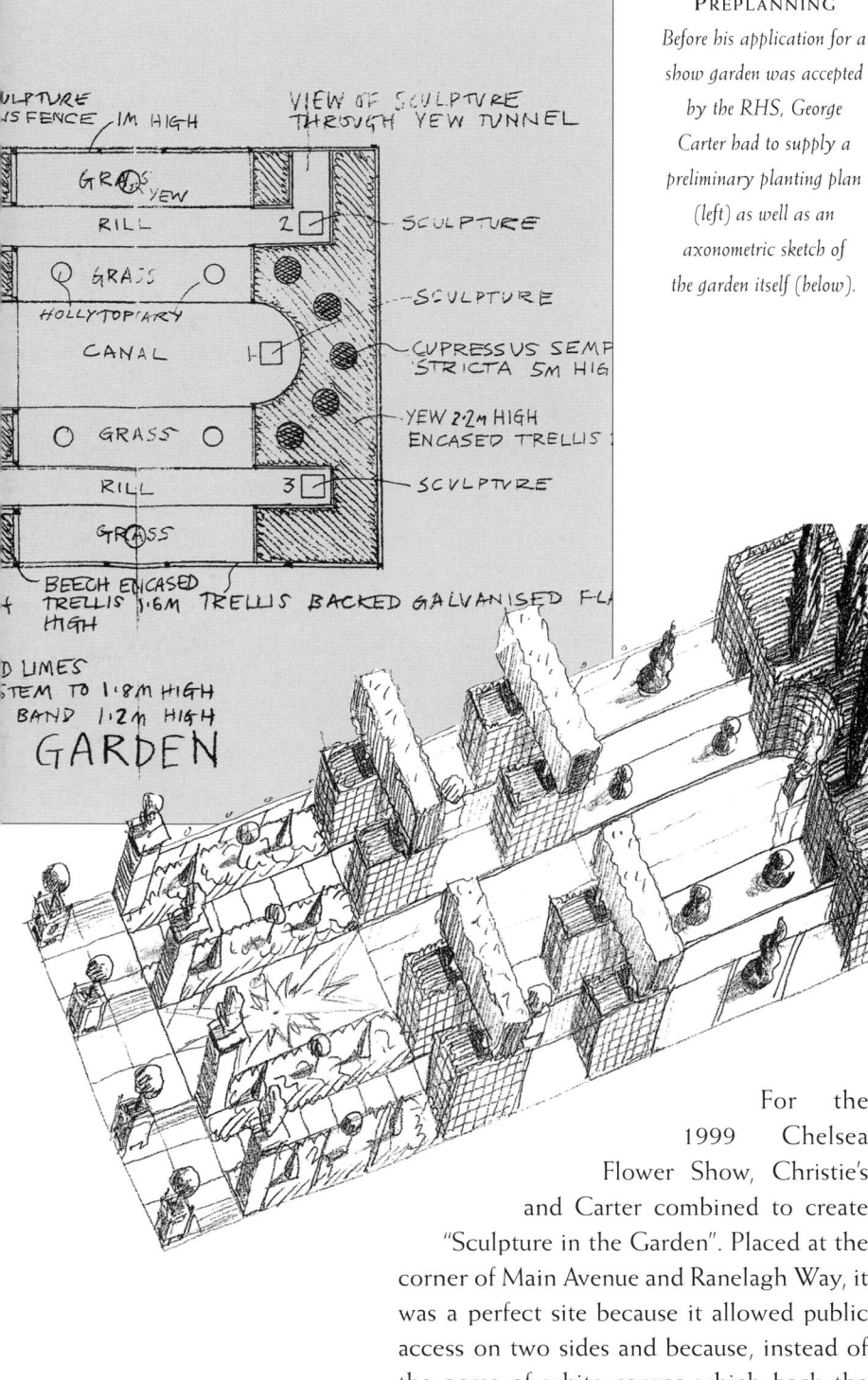

ULPTURE
IS FENCE IM HIGH

VIEW OF SCULPTURE
THROUGH YEW TUNNEL

GRASS
RILL   YEW
2

GRASS
HOLLYTOPIARY

CANAL   1

GRASS

RILL   3

GRASS

BEECH ENCASED
TRELLIS 1.6M TRELLIS BACKED GALVANISED FLA
HIGH

D LIMES
STEM TO 1.8M HIGH
BAND 1.2M HIGH

GARDEN

SCULPTURE

SCULPTURE

CUPRESSUS SEMP
STRICTA 5M HIG

YEW 2.2M HIGH
ENCASED TRELLIS

SCULPTURE

PREPLANNING
*Before his application for a
show garden was accepted
by the RHS, George
Carter had to supply a
preliminary planting plan
(left) as well as an
axonometric sketch of
the garden itself (below).*

For the
1999 Chelsea
Flower Show, Christie's
and Carter combined to create
"Sculpture in the Garden". Placed at the
corner of Main Avenue and Ranelagh Way, it
was a perfect site because it allowed public
access on two sides and because, instead of
the acres of white canvas which back the
gardens in front of the Great Marquee, it

had the mature plane trees of Ranelagh
Gardens at its rear.

"The 1999 garden was the responsibility
of myself and Caroline Clifton-Mogg,
Contributing Editor for *Christie's Magazine*,
and Graham Southern, Head of Christie's
Contemporary Art," explained Meredith
Etherington-Smith. "We wanted to sponsor a
garden mainly because our clients are
interested in gardens, and Chelsea is a very
effective publicity machine. Anyway, it is just
the sort of advertising we should be doing."

The most the auctioneers wanted to pay
for their Chelsea garden was £40,000 – and
by January 1999 they were already in
trouble. "We have problems," reported
Meredith Etherington-Smith, at the
start of an important meeting. "We just
cannot exceed the budget. We figure that
the far end of the garden is very costly in
terms of plants. Could the planting be
somehow altered to have fewer plants
or cheaper, smaller ones?"

"We could perhaps use trellis
backed with hessian instead of a
screen of plants," replied Carter,
with the calm that marks him out
from other more turbulent designers.
"Would the RHS dislike the idea of
using a canvas screen instead of plants?"
enquired Meredith Etherington-Smith.

Apparently other designers have put up
such screens and won Gold Medals in the
past. "Arabella Lennox-Boyd one year used a
yew hedge that was in fact branches of yew
stuck in the ground, which was, in theory,
against the rules," interjected Carter.

Perhaps it would be possible to replace
the massed, cut yews, which were designed
to make a tight dark finale to the garden,
with a scrim backing, using real plants only

on the area facing Ranelagh Way. Instead of pleached hornbeams overshadowing the planned sculpture, it might be possible to use parasol-shaped plane trees. "I've no experience of using planes," said Michael Miller from Clifton Nurseries, the show garden's contractor. "Will they come into leaf in time?"

"They would certainly provide a diffused light for the works of art," remarked Carter. "The light would be almost deliquescent."

"No leafless trees, please," pleaded Meredith Etherington-Smith. "Let's get on with looking at what we can do. Speed is of the essence at this stage."

Carter would phone Renato at Europlants, the Italian nursery that stocked mature trees and which frequently supplied them for gardens at Chelsea, to enquire about plane trees. Meanwhile Christie's would contact the major London art schools – among them the Royal College of Art, Chelsea School of Art, Goldsmiths', Camberwell, and St Martin's – to ask if they had any sculptors who could provide pieces for the show. Chelsea would be a major

showcase for any young sculptor, and Christie's wanted Chelsea visitors to realize that they had as keen an eye for the shock and controversy of the new art as for the value of the old masterpieces. "We wanted to make a corporate statement, to influence contemporary art in our own way," pointed out Christie's European Marketing Director Paul Hewitt.

"Choose lightweight sculptures," Carter advised Christie's show garden team. The last expense Christie's needed was the hire of heavyweight machinery to put the sculptures in place and then to worry about the dangers of subsidence or huge pieces of marble crushing onlookers. Nor was it a good idea to select works that needed wiring – many sculptures now rely on fibre-optic or neon lighting, which would be expensive.

PROGRESS MEETING

A month later, on a dismal February day, everyone met again at Christie's. Meredith Etherington-Smith reported the really shocking news that, apart from the Royal College of Art which was very keen, the only other art school that had answered her letter was Goldsmiths', which had asked for more information. "We wrote to ten, asking for their best students. Two replied, even though we made sure we wrote to the right person in each case. We may have to work with existing sculptures." Thus the unwitting students of eight art colleges had been denied an important public platform for their work.

The good news, on the other hand, was that Miller and Carter had managed to fit their costs to the budget. Against a maximum of £40,000, prices were currently standing at £35,950. This is how it was done: £200 was saved by reducing the cost of excavation because there were fewer trees than originally planned. Some £3,000 had been cut off the £11,000 bill for pleached trees by using eight parasol planes instead of pleached hornbeams. Each plane was to cost £300, but they would have to be delivered from Italy and might require a crane to lift them into place, depending on their size. Some £2,000 came off the £7,450 estimate for the end bed by using trellises and rusticated columns instead of plants, and by having a polythene screen

ANCIENT AND MODERN
Carter's design reinterpreted a classical, 17th-century sculpture garden in a 20th-century style by bringing together traditional formal topiary and contemporary sculpture.

behind the remaining yew trees, which would mask the white canvas backing on to the site. It was also hoped that the topiary for the lawns and shrub beds would be lent by the Romantic Garden Nursery, with whom Carter had a close relationship, as he had helped design their exhibitor's stands at previous shows. Such a loan would save £3,700. The beech topiary cubes in the plan would be replaced with box, saving £700. "We would stand a better chance of selling on the box rather than beech," Carter added.

The budget for the sculpture was then halved, to £500, by using existing works. Smaller trees also saved £500 on the £3,500 cost of dismantling the whole edifice at the end of the show. Renato in Italy had assured Carter that he could provide the parasol planes, and Carter thought that, instead of 8ft (2.5m) ones, 6ft (2m) tall yews at £75 each might be good enough. Carter himself could supply the four matching Versailles tubs, the sculpture pediments, and trellising from his own stock and paint them the correct grey.

These costs excluded VAT – and, more importantly, a design fee for Carter. There was insurance and printing charges to consider, too. "We should also stick on another £1,000 for lighting. The stand should be lit from 7.30pm, to impress visitors," said Miller.

"It's been a heroic effort," said Meredith Etherington-Smith, closing the meeting. "It is not at all easy on a shoestring. It's fine for people who can chuck masses of money at

REFLECTIVE BOAR
Neil Simmons's "Caledonian Boar", which was inspired by the famous bronze boar statue in Florence, attracted many admiring comments from visitors, including the Queen.

their gardens, and Chanel could afford to grow their beeches for three years. There is now talk about capping the cost of a show garden." Although this might be fairer when it came to awarding Gold Medals, it might cancel some of the really awe-inspiring efforts that have cost more than £100,000.

PUBLICITY FOR THE GARDEN

Caroline Clifton-Mogg then wrote an article on the planned show garden in *Christie's Magazine*. She recalled the enormous garden that surrounded the Villa of the Emperor Hadrian at Tivoli. "Over a vast acreage, works of sculptural art were placed, among colonnades, grottoes, and walks – an integral, indeed vital, element of the garden design. Each group, each placing was significant – not there merely for ornament's sake but as a religious and divine statement." She mentioned Pope Innocent VIII (1484–1492), whose Villa Belvedere outside Rome was a virtual open-air museum of sculpture, as well as Louis XIV who, with the designer André Le Nôtre (1613–1700), created a garden at Versailles, "the most

WEATHER WISE ▷
Because of lack of interest from most London art colleges in providing sculptures for the Christie's show garden in 1999, Carter designed his own sculptures. His theme was different weather conditions.

regal and complete expression of the formal garden in Europe".

"Christie's venture at Chelsea does not, surprisingly, aspire to the scale of the Sun King," wryly continued Caroline Clifton-Mogg's article. "Ours is a contemporary version of a formal garden, made the more contemporary because we will be displaying new works of sculpture, by young artists working today. The garden will be viewed from two sides, and on each side there will be vistas through, as well as water in the form of simple, black-lined canals that will give the necessary air of repose and stillness. Instead of colour – for a long time a dominant feature of many of the gardens at the Chelsea Flower Show – Christie's "Sculpture in the Garden" will instead use for contrast the play of light and dark, with plantings in soft neutral tones of greys and whites. Although following the classical principles of formal garden design, it will be intrinsically contemporary in nature. And in art."

In Christie's press release for the show, Carter wrote, "The garden re-interprets the 17th-century formal garden for the late 20th century. Surprisingly the baroque garden is often closer to modern minimalist gardens than 18th- and 19th-century 'naturalistic' ones. All the elements of the classic, late 17th-century garden are here – water, topiary, architecture, and sculpture – arranged to create an outdoor gallery with a series of exciting vistas."

LAST-MINUTE PROBLEMS

Everything was progressing well with the garden until two weeks before the show. Firstly, the temperature dropped suddenly and the plane trees, brought in from the balmier climate of Tuscany became frosted. Because they were so big, they had not fitted into the glasshouses at the site where they had been stored since their arrival in England, and someone (everyone was careful to make that someone anonymous) forgot to protect them with horticultural fleece overnight. A new set of eight plane trees had to be quickly imported from the Netherlands. They were bigger – and inevitably more expensive.

Secondly, the grey planting that George Carter had planned alongside the still, black canals then had to be radically changed, because specimens of the planned species were not good enough. No *Tanacetum densum* was available so quite different *T. niveum* 'Jackpot' was used instead. The medicinal sages, *Salvia officinalis*, had to be returned because they were not as big as the original sample, nor was *Hippophae rhamnoides* available in sufficiently large sizes, so *Senecio cineraria* and *Sedum* 'Herbstfreude' (synonym Autumn Joy) were substituted. Such last-minute changes always occur at Chelsea.

Once hung, the line of green hessian screening the back of the show garden looked pretty dreadful, even though it did conceal the white canvas behind. At the last minute, therefore, copper beeches were placed in front of the hessian. "For good photographs it is most important to hide the distracting paraphernalia of the show, particularly the white canvas structures and signs," Carter said. The pool edgings were also altered to improve the definition between the pale gravel of the paths and the black pool liner. One liner was too short, and had to be stretched to fit.

It proved very difficult to acquire suitable sculptures for the garden. The set of four that Carter wanted at the front of the garden were eventually made by him. Neil Simmons's plaster and painted-stone "Caledonian Boar", similar to the wild boar statue in Florence, took the prime position, sitting serenely and impressively at the centre back of the garden, reflected in the silent pool. His sculpture had originally been made for English Heritage at Osborne House on the Isle of Wight. The Queen, when she visited Carter's garden, pointed out that there are copies everywhere, including Balmoral.

Georgina Miller's "The Hyaline" – two chrome-plated aluminium casts mounted on glass cases – was ready in time for the show, but Olivia Musgrave's two bronzes, of "Apollo & Daphne" and "Orpheus", were stolen from her studio only days before the Chelsea Flower Show opened. She found them in a scrapyard the day they were due to be collected by Christie's – and did not tell anyone about the traumatic drama until the end of the show, by which time "Sculpture in the Garden" had won a well-deserved Gold Medal. It had also come in just below the agreed budget of £40,000.

"We were very happy – delighted – with the Gold," said Hewitt after the event, "but it is a hard act to follow and we probably won't exhibit again for a few years."

PEACEFUL SETTING

Throughout the garden, textural surfaces, trees, and box topiary were used to reflect light and to accentuate the shapes of the contemporary sculptures.

THE SHOWMEN

" There's something unique about the show: it's like having a baby – it is wonderful when it stops. It's just the best in the world. "

LONG TRADITION
A few firms, such as Hillier, have exhibited ever since the first Chelsea Flower Show, in 1913.

DENIS O'BRIEN BAKER who died in 2003 aged 88, was probably the longest-serving exhibitor at Chelsea. He was there as a schoolboy in 1933, and two years later he was helping on Perry's stands, when he remembered seeing George V tour the show with Queen Mary, who wore a long coat and toque. He also recollected the days before the Great Marquee was first erected, in 1951. "There were two tents before then, the East Marquee and the West Marquee."

The 1933 Chelsea was held only 15 years after the First World War had ended – a war that had changed society enormously – yet Baker recalled that the Chelsea Flower Show was still the official opening of the London Season. Even if the crowds of society ladies and their aristocratic husbands knew or cared little about gardening, they made sure they were at this fashionable event.

Two years later, in 1935, Baker was a staff member on the Perry's stands. "There were no island stands, then," he recalled. "It was very old-fashioned, with lines and lines of exhibitors on long tables. The public could not always recognize where one exhibitor ended and another started, so it was very unsatisfactory." The show was dominated by the major nurseries such as Allwoods, which had huge stands of pinks and carnations, and by the seeds merchants. Most visitors were immensely grand and owned estates of many acres, but the true gardening expertise lay with their head gardeners, who would buy from the seedsmen at Chelsea to propagate their own plants.

"The first day was a fashion show. It was just the same as Ascot, with ladies in fancy hats. Some of the

To celebrate their 125 years of business, Hillier Nurseries proudly displayed on their 1989 stand some of the many awards they had won over seven decades at Chelsea.

▽ CLEAN SWEEP

Gardeners at Chelsea come in all shapes and sizes. This one, on the Gardeners' World stand in 1995, was made of woven willow branches, more generally employed for baskets and hurdles.

men even wore top hats," Baker went on. Most of the rest wore bowlers, Panamas, trilbies, and homburgs. "In the first two days we didn't take many orders because generally the gardeners came later."

Perry's had two separate stands: one of large waterside plants such as *Gunnera manicata*, and another of alpines. "I worked on both," said Baker. "I wasn't an apprentice. The system then was better than an apprenticeship: I worked the same hours and was paid the same rate as the more experienced men and I learnt by watching the others while I was sweeping up." In 1937 he joined Notcutts – a firm that has exhibited at Chelsea from the first show – where he

worked on their Chelsea stand for three shows.

In 1939 Baker set up his own firm, Home Meadows Nursery, with his wife, whom he had met at Perry's. From then they exhibited their Iceland poppies at virtually every Chelsea, until his wife died in 1999. Baker believed that the type of people who visited the Chelsea Flower Show changed greatly after the Second World War. "It became a cosmopolitan crowd and no one was tremendously dressed up. People were also more knowledgeable, gardening themselves rather than leaving their estates solely to the gardener."

Home Meadows is still a family firm, with Baker's son and daughter now showing at Chelsea, although Baker always came for at least one day each year. Each Chelsea, they sell thousands of seed packets to, he believed, virtually every country in the world. "We simply go to Chelsea for the trade. It has been very helpful that we can sell seed direct from the stand – it's only been allowed for the last few years – because it is so expensive to take a note of each enquiry and send it on."

With his six decades of experience as a Chelsea exhibitor, Baker had strong views about how the show is run. One major flaw, he believed, was the one-way system in the Great Marquee. "People should be free to go where they want. I don't think herding people like sheep was a success." He would also have liked a bit more information from the judges. "You do not always get a straight answer on why they've given you this or that medal. It would be nice if they could be a little more outgoing to the exhibitors." He was not too keen on the current trend in show gardens, either; yet on the whole the Chelsea Flower Show had his approval. "Maybe it does need a shake-up now and again, but Chelsea has been as good as ever from the business point of view. There's no other show like it."

CHANGES AT CHELSEA

Another family-run firm that has a long history of exhibiting at Chelsea is Hillier Nurseries. In fact it had a stand at the very first Chelsea Flower Show, in 1913. Its President, John Hillier, is also Chairman of the current RHS panel for the Chelsea floral tent. "I can remember my father saying that, between the wars, people came with their gardeners but that changed after the Second World War," recalled Hillier. "Inter-war, quite a number of visitors placed orders at our stand and then cancelled them the next day because they'd been showing off in front of their friends. We used to take orders for 9ft [2.8m] or 10ft [3m] standard trees, which with their roots were 13–14ft [4.3–4.7m] when packed in bundles for the railway. I can remember the old packing sheds at our

nurseries in the 1950s and early 1960s, when the railway lorry collected packages, often twice a day from October to April, to take to the local station for delivery by train on to their various destinations.

"Perhaps the biggest change at Chelsea is that our stand is now better designed due to our changed emphasis, from retail mail-order nursery to wholesale grower with 12 retail garden centres," Hillier went on. "In my father's day we placed as many plants as possible on the stand, as our core business was selling rare and unusual plants directly to gardeners. Now, with garden centres predominating, our stand combines plants with gardening accessories such as structures, which we also now sell. We still however use plants in a similar way to a painter experimenting with paints from his palette.

"With the new structure we can't have such a tall display, as the ceiling is only about 20ft [6m] tall. At its highest the Great Marquee was more than 30ft [10m], though in the valleys there was only 10ft [3m] to the base. With a display of 4,050sq ft [375sq m] – 45ft [13.7m] by 90ft [27.4m] – we do need height. The new arrangements are an interesting challenge."

BEGONIA BREEDER
At Blackmore & Langdon's nursery in the mid 1970s, Stephen Langdon selects begonias from among those he himself had bred, for inclusion on the firm's annual stand at Chelsea.

DOUBLE DUTY

Gardeners at Blackmore & Langdon pose in front of the horse-drawn van in which they transported all their exhibits during the early years, and where they would sleep during the show's duration.

SPECIALIST NURSERYMEN

Blackmore & Langdon, of Pensford, near Bristol, is another survivor of those first Chelsea years. Among their many Gold Medals is one from the precursor of Chelsea, the Royal International Horticultural Exhibition of 1912. The firm was formed in 1901 by J.B. Blackmore, an engineer/publican who was an enthusiastic amateur begonia grower, and Charles Langdon, a head gardener. Its early fortunes were founded on a sensational delphinium, 'Reverend E. Lascelles', which was named after the wealthy vicar for whom Charles Langdon had been head gardener. Blackmore & Langdon have continued to show their famous delphiniums at Chelsea, along with prize begonias, although 'Reverend E. Lascelles' disappeared in about 1960. They have won 60–70 Gold Medals since the first Chelsea Flower Show, recalled John Langdon, the third generation of Langdons to exhibit at Chelsea. "There are no members of the Blackmore family left in the company – the last one, Tom, died in 1972," he explained, "so the company is now run by myself, my wife

Rosemary, and our three sons, Simon, Stephen, and Nicholas."

The firm exhibits at about 18 shows every year. "The begonias and delphiniums are packed into our own vans, and it takes us only a few hours to reach the showgrounds. It is hard to believe that, in the early days, the plants were packed into a horse-drawn box van with iron wheels and no suspension, and pulled to the railway station over cobbled streets. The van was next loaded on to the train and taken to the station nearest the showground, and then again pulled by horses to its destination. When the van was unloaded, the staff would use it as their sleeping quarters, the only beds being the straw that was used to pack the begonias – all rather different to the caravan with hot shower and other facilities we use today."

The importance of Blackmore & Langdon and their displays at Chelsea was emphasized by Colin Edwards in his book *Delphiniums: The Complete Guide*. "It is hard to exaggerate the tremendous influence that this nursery has had on the improvement and popularity of the delphinium. There can be few visitors to the Chelsea Flower Show who are not astonished by their magnificent display."

The firm has been just as influential with begonias. In *The Tuberous Begonia* Brian Langdon related how Blackmore & Langdon caused a sensation in Ghent in 1913 and, the same year, were also at Chelsea. Their prize begonia of that year – salmon-pink 'Princess Victoria Louise' – was considered revolutionary, because of the size of the blooms (almost 5in/12cm across) and the much-improved, rose-shaped centres. Hitherto begonia lovers had been familiar only with the mass-produced, smaller-flowered bedding varieties.

Both Charles Langdon and his son Allan were awarded the Victoria Medal of Honour by the RHS.

SHOW EXHIBITS

Delphiniums were an early speciality for Blackmore & Langdon. Here staff, in the mid 1980s, tie exhibition plants to their supports, in the nursery (above). Their perfect delphiniums (right) always draw gasps of admiration from the Chelsea crowds, whose appreciation would be even greater if they realized the problems of growing and transporting such prize-winning blooms.

DELPHINIUM

CONSPICUOUS

PREPARING THE PLANTS

MANY VISITORS WALKING around the Great Pavilion may wonder how exhibitors manage to make plants from so many different seasons — daffodils, roses, lupins, cauliflowers, bluebells, and geraniums — all flower during the same week in May. It is easy to forget how unnatural the whole affair is when all the plants look so perfectly formed, so healthy, and natural. The herbaceous borders are so luscious; the vegetable stalls resemble a harvest festival; the roses, at their summer peak, are twined around pergolas; and ferns are thrusting up on the same stand as flowering pelargoniums.

What has happened, in the depths of winter and the long, dark nights, is that nurserymen have been persuading their plants to perform for this one week only, by making them react as if it were the right time of year for them to flower or fruit.

TRICKS OF THE TRADE

Maurice Woodfield, of Woodfield Bros (specialists in lupins), explained how his firm prepares for the Chelsea Flower Show. Lupins generally flower in the summer, so Woodfield's particular challenge is to ensure that the blooms on their exhibits are at their peak in late May, just for the judging day at the Chelsea Flower Show. "We grow all our own plants. Under glass, we take about 1,800 lupin cuttings in February and March, some 15 months before the show. We gradually pot them on until they are in 10in (25cm) pots, by October, when we stand them outside. In late January the pots are brought into the greenhouses again.

"With 16 years' experience we can then assess which ones have a chance of making Chelsea. Depending on the weather in the run-up to the show, we have to keep the plants cooler or warmer, heating up the greenhouse when it is cold and putting them outside if it's hot. In 1998 we had to reduce to half a stand at the show because the plants were flooded at Easter. By April we have 300–400 lupins waiting for Chelsea, because once the lupins start to tassel up, or flower, they can't be stopped. We like to take 160–170 plants to the show, of which 150 will make it to the stand. We load the vans very tightly so that all the plants interlock and, fortunately, none has ever been damaged.

"To us all the hard work to achieve a good Chelsea display is thoroughly worthwhile, as we've always been addicted to lupins ever since we were small lads."

ROSE EXPERTS

Another exhibitor at Chelsea is Michael Marriott, of David Austin Roses (specialists in roses). "We grow twice the number of plants for Chelsea than we need. There might be 350 on the stand, so between 600 and 700 are prepared. In January we partially repot all plants intended for the show in fresh compost containing slow-release

PERFECTED ART

Woodfield Bros are leaders in the world of modern lupins. Their perfect flowers are notable for fine colour and because the whole spire matures at once. Previous varieties tended to die back from the bottom.

fertilizer and anti-vine weevil compound. Initially we keep the plants at a minimum of about 41°F (5°C), allowing the sun to promote growth. We do not want to force the roses too far too early as it may be warm later on and then it is almost impossible to hold them back.

"Our greenhouses are divided into three areas, each with its own temperature regime. We can also put the plants into a shaded area outside, to hold them back. We have grown many of our varieties for many years so know whether they flower early or late, and how much forcing they need. Each season is different, of course, and so we juggle the plants between each of the areas, aiming to achieve the maximum number of flowers exactly on time for Chelsea. If any roses are particularly slow, we keep them at a high temperature in the greenhouse on a damp floor with high light levels. You have to be careful, though, when forcing roses: they change shape and colour and do not look representative, or they flop.

"Watering is crucial: if the plants are allowed to dry out they become more susceptible to powdery mildew and their flower development also radically slows down. Watering is done by hand, because this ensures that every plant is looked at intimately almost every day. The most crucial time is the last two weeks or so before the show opens, when the buds are just about bursting. If it is very sunny and warm, they can easily open too quickly and so be over for the actual show. The 1999 Chelsea was one of the easiest I remember, because everything grew at a steady pace.

"On the Wednesday before Chelsea we do a mock-up of the stand in the shed. The next day each chosen plant is wrapped in brown

paper and put on to lorries, which travel overnight to arrive by 8am on the Friday.

"We keep our roses from year to year. We think they have more character than new plants. After the show, they are put back in the greenhouse and fed, watered, and sprayed regularly until the following January, when the cycle starts all over again."

CROWD DUST

One problem at Chelsea, according to David Austin Roses, is that it is very dry in the pavilion, and all the people gradually create a layer of dust, which settles on the roses (and the lungs). Roses look even worse if they are washed down, so their staff have to ignore the dust.

SKILFUL CULTIVATION

The Chelsea preparation time for Ursula Key-Davis, of Fibrex Nurseries (specialists in pelargoniums, ivies, and hardy ferns), is longer than for David Austin Roses. "We start thinking about what to do about the July before the show and prepare about three times the number of plants we will finally need. From some 2,500–3,000 plants we select the best 1,190, which we replant. To achieve the complete look you would expect when grown to maturity, we overplant a series of differently sized bowls, which encourages plants of various heights and so gives definition to our stand. Some 22 bowls, 30in [75cm] wide, are crammed with 20 pelargoniums each (normally you'd only plant about eight to a pot). Then we use 20 smaller bowls, 18in [45cm] wide, which take nine plants each. There are also 50 bowls, 8in [20cm] wide, each with three scented-leaf pelargoniums; as well as 70 hanging baskets, 9in [23cm] wide, holding six plants each.

REGULAR EXHIBITS
The ferns used for Chelsea are returned to this polytunnel between shows.

"We plant up the hanging baskets in October, because this gives the plants extra time to mature. We force the Regal and Zonal pelargoniums into flower by about a month in advance of their normal flowering time (June) by giving them high potash feeds and no nitrogen. We have several small greenhouses – with different areas in each, offering varied light conditions and temperatures – and we move the plants from one to another, as necessary. If the season is early, they go in cold greenhouses and vice versa. From experience we now know which plants to pick and where to move them. It sometimes works and sometimes doesn't.

"It can still go wrong. When we had a mild winter beforehand, the atmosphere under glass became very humid as we were reaching the last stages, causing damping off in the bloom on some plants, which therefore could not be used for the show.

◁ **WATER CONTROL**
Ursula Key-Davis has had years of experience in how and when to water pelargoniums, so that they are at their best for the Chelsea Flower Show.

"The ivies and ferns on the stand are treated in a similar way to the pelargoniums except that these have to be forced very gently so as not to make the foliage too soft, which renders them useless on the stand as they are unable to tolerate the journey or necessary handling during staging. We never buy-in ivies or ferns as there is no one else who grows the varieties that we require.

"We've had 30 years' experience of coping with Chelsea, but to us it is very worthwhile, because it is the show window for the horticultural world."

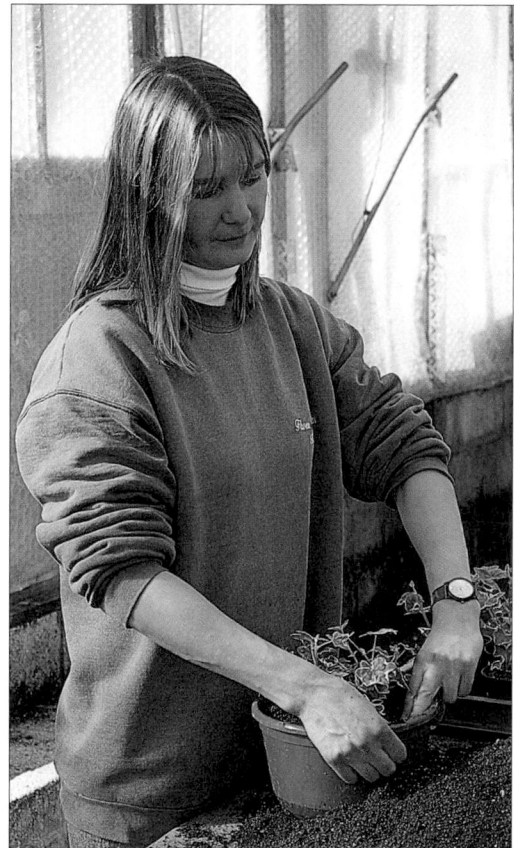

△ POTTING PLANTS

Ten months before Chelsea, the pelargoniums for the show are replanted more densely than the others, to speed maturity.

STOCKROOM ▷
Many of the possible plants for inclusion in Hillier's Chelsea displays are kept in glasshouses. Here Ricky Dorlay prunes a potential exhibit so that it retains its well-balanced shape.

STAR ATTRACTION
Among the plants Hillier had prepared for Chelsea 2000 was this Solanum laxum *'Album', with its long and reliable flowering period.*

ANNUAL CYCLE

Hillier Nurseries also have considerable experience of showing at Chelsea, having exhibited every year since the first show in 1913. In 2003 the Hampshire nursery, world famous for trees and shrubs, was awarded its 57th consecutive Chelsea Gold Medal.

According to Andrew McIndoe, Deputy Managing Director and designer of the Hillier exhibit, planning starts for the next year as soon as Chelsea is over. "Once I have decided on a theme and colour scheme, I start to plan what plants will be required. For the 1999 show I included a 'Green Garden', which incorporated 'green' material such as crushed recycled glass and painted household containers alongside the green and variegated foliage of trees, shrubs, and climbers. White

roses, lilies, and tulips provided the seasonal interest. For Chelsea 2000, I did a "Tea Garden for the 21st Century", using aromatic plants and those with a strong tea connection: camellias, roses, and jasmine, for example.

"Growing for Chelsea does require careful planning ahead. There is no point deciding in November that I would like a 6ft (2m) *Jasminum officinalis*. It just will not put on enough growth by the following May.

"Chelsea plants are grown alongside normal crops at our main production nursery. Heated glasshouses are used to force roses and later-flowering herbaceous perennials. Although we resort to cold storage to hold plants back, we avoid it if at all possible. Azaleas and rhododendrons, for example, do not react well to hot weather during the show

if they have previously been in the cold store. The majority of plants selected are those that naturally look good at the time. Some rose varieties perform well, especially small-flowered types such as 'Ballerina' and BONICA ('Meidomonac'). White Flower Carpet™ and ICEBERG ('Korbin') used in 1999 both performed brilliantly." About 3,000 plants are put in the exhibit, although about 4,000 are prepared by Ricky Dorlay, Hillier's showman of more than 30 years.

Hillier's prefer to stage plants by eye to create a more natural effect. "We do not plan the exact position of plants in advance," commented McIndoe. "We take them along to the show and decide then and there. We can always tell gardens that have been limited by the designer."

TREE NURSERY ▷

Large trees, some 20ft (6m) or more tall, are grown in containers, for successful transplanting. In the nursery they are attached to horizontal wires, as here, so they are supported against strong winds.

VEGETABLE KING

According to Medwyn Williams, of Medwyn's (specialists in vegetables), "my whole aim when I started to come to Chelsea was to prove that I could create August and September in May. It was critical to know my sowing dates and to give the plants artificial lighting and heat. I need to sow leeks in July, onions in August, and carrots and parsley in mid-December." This is at least six months earlier than most gardeners sow their vegetables in the UK. "Then, in January, I sow most other vegetables, such as beetroot,

ROOT VEGETABLES

Medwyn's grow long carrots, mooli, parsnips, and beetroot in 4ft (1.2m) pipes, 6in (15cm) in diameter and filled with sand, peat, and vermiculite. About 18 pipes might produce one good carrot, and at least a dozen are needed on a Chelsea stand. The firm allows a margin of roughly 30 per cent extra for spoilage, and even then they sometimes have only just enough.

PEERLESS POTATOES

Medwyn Williams checks his potatoes in their unheated greenhouse. He exhibits seven varieties of potatoes alone.

Tuscan black cabbage, and tomatoes. Last of all are the radishes, which go in towards the end of March. To trick the vegetables that it is the end of summer (when most are in peak condition), you need 16 hours' lighting and a temperature of 65°F (19°C) right through the growing season.

"It all started when I was asked to judge at Chelsea and I just thought I can do better than that. I've succeeded by trial and error. My first Chelsea was in 1996 but I had kept diaries with growing details about the run-up to horticultural shows throughout the country at which I had exhibited regularly in August and September, and I used these to work out a timetable for forcing vegetables for showing at Chelsea. I've been lucky with nearly everything – only the peas and broad beans let me down by maturing early – and I

IMMACULATE DISPLAY ▷

One of the consistently enjoyable sights is Medwyn's annual display of gigantic and regimented vegetables from yard-long leeks to strange coloured carrots.

failed again with them in 1999, short by only ten days. But still, I had a lovely meal of them when I got back from the show.

"I've never won anything less than a Gold Medal. I also received a Gold Medal at the Cincinnati Show at the end of April 1999, although I didn't have a permit to show there until the week before I left home. At the end of that show, everything had to be incinerated in case a little Welsh dragon was let loose in America. Sometimes I think you have to be mad to exhibit."

△ ONION CARE

Each size and type of vegetable requires a different forcing technique. Small onions, for example, are grown from sets in 2 litre rose pots on benches in a greenhouse.

AN EXHIBITOR'S VIEW

WHY DO NURSERYMEN exhibit at the Chelsea Flower Show? The lead-up can last a year, if not longer, and is exhausting – and such nurserymen generally have a full-time day job running their regular businesses, too. They find the five days of the show incredibly tiring, and yet immediately after one show ends these showmen are planning for the next. That's not to mention the stress that such a competition brings: if you are awarded a Silver Medal while a competing specialist acquires a Gold, you may well lose business and you'll certainly lose heart, especially when you have to remain at the show with everyone knowing about it. It can also be difficult, day after day, to be faced with thousands of expert gardeners, all poring over your stand for long hours, asking questions and generally commenting.

CAREFUL PLANNING

Jekka McVicar draws a meticulous plan of how each of her herbs will be displayed. By the end of May, a week after she has packed up the currant show, she was already working on her design for the stand in the next year.

I therefore asked award-winning Jekka McVicar, who founded her own herb nursery in the 1980s, what was the attraction of exhibiting at the show. She has been at Chelsea for the last seven years and, in that time, has earned no less than four Gold Medals and three Silver-Gilts for her herbs. She wasn't even bred to gardening; she was a television programme director until she gave it all up for herbs. She is helped at Chelsea by her husband, who takes his annual holidays each May.

Like all first-timers, she found her debut to be full of pitfalls, probably because she had never before encountered the organized chaos, the long traffic queues of vans unloading supplies, the cranes, the teams of helpers on every stand, and the snaking water pipes and electric wires. It has to be experienced to be believed.

"My first year I didn't realize there'd be no space for the ramp on my horsebox – the cars during the build-up are nose to tail – and we also thought we had until Monday lunchtime to get ready," recalled Jekka McVicar. "No one told us the press came round on Monday morning."

"The days before we pack for each show are always awful," Jekka McVicar continued. "Depending on the weather, I can be up at 3am in my nightie, taking stock in and out of the polytunnels. If it is freezing, I'll be out there protecting the herbs with horticultural

HERBAL HARVEST

Jekka McVicar grows all her own plants for exhibiting at the Chelsea Flower Show. Here she tends them at her nursery, which is in the country, near Bristol.

fleece. If snow is forecast, the whole lot – at least 200 plants – will have to be brought into the polytunnels."

Even in Jekka McVicar's first year, the Queen and the Duke of Edinburgh stopped at her stand. She had been told that they never stopped at beginners' stands and had made no plans about how to deal with such a situation. "It was really noticeable how knowledgeable they were. In 1993 I had a Scottish plant called baldmoney (*Meum athamanticum*), and the Queen turned to the Duke and said, 'Darling do we have it up there [meaning Balmoral]?' Another year she liked the asparagus pea in flower."

During the show, Jekka McVicar sleeps in her own caravan in Battersea Park. "I arrive with my husband the Thursday before the show opens, and he goes home on the Sunday," she said. From Battersea Park she can nip across the river to keep an eye on the stand and the condition of the plants. "It's essential to be able to go in when I want. I'm there from 8am to 8pm every day the show is open, and then I water the herbs before leaving at about 9.45pm. On the Tuesday, I'm there at 6am to see if I've won a medal and then I have breakfast. I know I won't eat anything again that day. I can't leave the stand – I even have to wait to go to the toilet – it's an ordeal."

"I hate the last Friday of Chelsea – it's like destroying an illusion. I don't sell my stock, so I just tell people who want to buy plants from the stand to go away. When the show is over, I pack everything up and drive my caravan home at 3am. It takes me two days to unload everything."

To counterbalance such hard work and stress when exhibiting at the show, there are obvious advantages, especially to those who

win so consistently: your name is made, and your sales go up. For Jekka McVicar, however, the Chelsea Flower Show has a magic unlike any other – an atmosphere at once so friendly and imposing that she cannot describe it. "There is no other show like Chelsea. It is small and condensed, and it is only medals from Chelsea that people really remember. Nearly half the exhibitors are small firms – just husband and wife teams like us, for whom the show is a way of life," explained Jekka McVicar. "There's something unique about the show: it's like having a baby – it is wonderful when it stops. It's just the best in the world."

FLOWERING HERBS

Herbs can be very rewarding to exhibit, especially if they are left to flower. Chives, which once were ruthlessly de-flowered so as to preserve the oniony leaves at their best, are now recognized for their floral value (as here) as well as their delicious taste.

THERE FROM THE START

NOTCUTTS OF WOODBRIDGE is one of only three nurseries to have exhibited at every Chelsea Flower Show since the very first, in 1913 – the other two being Blackmore & Langdon and Hillier Nurseries. Each firm is still family-run.

Thomas Wood started a nursery at Woodbridge in 1749. In 1784 François de la Rouchefoucauld, when on a tour of England, visited the nursery and reported dismissively, "I saw nothing but two nursery gardens near the town, one of 9 acres [3.6 hectares] and the other 4 or 5 acres [1.6 or 2 hectares]. They were full of small green

trees, some of which were priced very low." By 1895 the nursery had a list of 95 apple varieties, 35 pears, 25 plums, and no less than 123 roses. Two years later John Wood, whose family had run the nursery for almost 150 years, died without heirs. The whole nursery was bought in 1897 by Roger Crompton Notcutt (always known as RCN), who already, in his teens, had acquired a nursery at Broughton Road in Ipswich, about 9 miles from Woodbridge.

RCN was 28 when he expanded into Woodbridge, moving into the attractive Georgian house on the nursery with his wife, Maud. During his career he was a member of the RHS Shows Committee for 30 years, was in the Linnean Society, and on

AWARD-WINNING YEARS

Notcutts have exhibited successfully at the Chelsea Flower Show since its inception, in 1913. In 1988 they celebrated their 75th appearance, with a special display.

△ **WORKING IN WATER**

This early 20th-century water garden in Notcutts' Woodbridge Nursery was one of several display borders that were used to stock plants for propagation, to grow plants for exhibition, and to show potential customers what young plants look like when mature.

THE VERY BEST DISPLAY ▷

Although they initially exhibited in the open part of the showground, Notcutts later moved into the Great Marquee, where they produced eye-catching displays of trees, shrubs, and perennials, as here in 1994. This particular garden not only won a Gold Medal but also the Lawrence Medal for the best exhibit at any RHS show during the whole of 1994.

the Council of the Roads Beautifying Association, an early environmental lobby group. He served on the Council of the Suffolk Preservation Society, and in 1934 gave the National Trust its first donation in Suffolk, Kyson Hill, with its splendid views of the River Deben.

RCN was the perfect example of a committed nurseryman at the time of the first Chelsea, in 1913. He was accustomed to exhibiting at the Inner Temple shows and had attended the 1912 Royal International Horticultural Exhibition, where his nursery had gained a Silver-Gilt Medal for its rose

UNUSUAL OBELISK

During the Chelsea Flower Show this memorial has had displays built around it, such as this one by Notcutts in 1999. In that year a tribute was paid by the Royal Regiment of Wales to their predecessors who died during the 1849 Chillianwallah battle, in the Second Sikh War.

garden. In 1914 Notcutts won their first Gold Medal – for an azalea garden. This was the first of many, usually Gold, Medals acquired by Notcutts for their impressive displays of roses, shrubs, and trees at the Chelsea Flower Show.

"We have RCN's medals and catalogues, but all his papers have disappeared, so there are no other historical archives," explained RCN's grandson, Charles, who was born in 1934. Charles Notcutt is the current Chairman of Notcutts, as well as holder of a Victoria Medal of Honour and an RHS Council member for ten years, until 1999.

"I started going to Chelsea in 1956 – as a student, helping – and I was back in 1958, after I'd joined the family firm," continued Notcutt. "At that time the Great Marquee was dominated by the large seed firms – Suttons, Carters, and Webbs – with their huge exhibits. They all withdrew in the 1960s, with the arrival of garden centres and the disappearance of employed gardeners. Another major shift in the character of the pavilions has been the demise of the large displays by Belgium and the Netherlands and the arrival of exhibits from Kirstenbosch (the South African National Botanical Institute) and the Caribbean Islands. There has also been a reduction in the number of displays by large municipal parks such as Torbay and Birmingham, and it was very sad when the newly privatized Royal London Parks had to pull out in the 1980s, because of lack of money. Birmingham fortunately has been able to continue exhibiting at Chelsea, by raising sponsorship. Many small, more specialist exhibitors have taken the place of these large ones."

An even more important change in the 1960s, Notcutt remembered, "came when

CHANGING STYLES
To publicize their garden centres, Notcutts every year re-create a superb garden on an enormous site in the Great Marquee. For the 1988 show, for example they designed a rustic-style garden (left), while signs of the emerging fashion for exotic planting appeared in their 1991 display (right).

the country was frozen between Boxing Day 1962 and early March 1963. Plants in people's gardens all over the country were killed that winter, so the public poured into Chelsea to try to replace them; on the Thursday afternoon the Chairman of the RHS Shows Committee, John Russell, nearly had to close the show gates because of the crowds.

"During that 1962/63 winter, orders that had already been placed with mail-order nurseries could not be dug up for dispatch, and many nurseries had so many orders in hand that they were unable to accept new business in the spring." The public therefore began to discover how convenient garden centres were for the immediate purchase and collection of plants. "In that year, the concept of garden centres really started to become popular," Notcutt went on. "Until then, nearly all plant sales had been by mail order, delivered by our own lorries or by public carrier. We used to take orders at the show for delivery in the autumn, but most of the large nurseries have now ceased to do that. The trend towards the use of garden centres was

there before the 1963 Chelsea but that particular show increased the momentum."

Since then plants have been sold in containers and all year round, rather than being available bare-rooted or rootballed, only in spring or autumn. Consequently, for nurserymen, the role of Chelsea has changed radically. "Hilliers and ourselves now exhibit for general publicity, particularly on television. That is the whole purpose for us being there," Notcutt said.

What of the future? "It's worrying," ventured Notcutt, "because there's this image of overcrowding at Chelsea, even though the Hampton Court show has been reducing the pressure during the 1990s. At Hampton Court there are now over 180,000 visitors to Chelsea's 160,000, and the advantage at Hampton Court is that people can buy and collect plants at the show. Chelsea does not have that arrangement. It is a traditional flower show, yet the prestige is so high that exhibitors feel they must be there. We have to hope that in future with the new marquees there will be less congestion, less pressure, and more pleasure. The show must evolve."

THE SOCIAL SIDE

" It's an opportunity to see the very best garden design in Britain – an unbeatable resource of ideas and inspiration. "

CONTRASTING COLOURS
Dan Pearson used Verbascum *'Cotswold Queen' and* Iris *'Kent Pride' in his "Vibrant London Garden", in 1994.*

WHY DO BUSINESSES as diverse as Chanel, Schroders, *Harpers & Queen*, and Mercury Asset Management invest in the Chelsea Flower Show? The answer is that they want to ally themselves with all that Chelsea implies: tradition, the opening of the London Season, high-quality gardening, and exclusivity. Such companies sponsor a show garden or buy tickets for the Gala Preview, held on the Monday evening after the Royal Visit. The hefty catalogue of the Gala Preview, in which all firms who buy tickets are able to take a full-page advertisement, features the grandest names. Major sponsors of the Gala Preview have been: Enterprise Oil in 1989, 1990, 1992, and 1993; EMI in 1991 and 1997; Safeway in 1994; Touche Ross and its successor Deloitte & Touche in 1995 and 1998; and the corporate financiers

Hawkpoint Partners in 1999 and PricewaterhouseCoopers in 2000. Merrill Lynch Investment Managers (MLIM) were the sponsers in 2001 and Merrill Lynch (ML) since then, with Peter Gibbs, Global Chief Operating Officer, writing in 2001: "Since becoming involved with the Chelsea Flower Show, we have quickly discovered that gardening and investment management share many similarities; success in both fields requires a huge amount of research, planning, attention to detail, creativity and the ability to produce excellent results whatever the climate."

The Gala Preview at Chelsea is probably the biggest regular, annual, fund-raising event in Britain today, with all of its profits going to charity. Tickets cost from £225 and are more sought after than those for the Wimbledon tennis championships – they are

generally sold out to firms a year in advance. "The Gala Preview allows about 5,000 people to see the show before the crowds arrive. On each RHS members' or public day some 40,000 people pass through the gates," Former Chelsea caterers, Gardner Merchant's Regional Director Russell Haddon commented. "We serve more glasses of champagne here than at any other event handled by our Town & County division." After the early evening Gala Preview, the exclusive hospitality chalets are used for celebration dinner parties by the big city firms. "We cater for about 1,000 dinners and afterwards we have to bring in an overnight crew of 50 to re-set the chalets ready for 8am the next day, when the RHS members arrive."

Janet O'Hara of Acaria runs sponsorship and event management for Schroders. The occasions that she organizes vary from rugby and cricket matches through to art events, but Chelsea is easily the most popular, because of its exclusivity. "The most senior directors take Gala Preview tickets for their most important clients – the chairmen and the chief executives. The demand for tickets is incredible: four or five months before the event, clients start hinting about tickets. We could use double the allowance. Chelsea is a special invitation, very much in demand."

This view was endorsed by the New York socialite Wendy Breck, who came to the 1999 Gala Preview. "What I've seen here makes the San Francisco, the Philadelphia, and the Washington flower shows look like chopped liver."

FRENCH FORMALITY

Harpers & Queen *and Cartier sponsored this symmetrical garden, which was entitled "Classical Garden" and designed by Michael Miller in 1994.*

◁ TRUST CENTENARY

To celebrate the National Trust's centenary in 1995, Arabella Lennox-Boyd created a garden inspired by the Lake District, using old slate walls and fountains. Financed by the Daily Telegraph, *two yew trees and an arch framed an antique urn.*

ATTRACTING THE RIGHT BUSINESS
Sponsorship of the show gardens is equally prestigious. The fashion house Chanel admitted spending around £50,000 on a single garden in 1998. Director of Public Relations and Fashion Bernadette Rendall said she was drawn to the idea because "Chelsea is a big, big

event. The garden was designed in the Chanel style. We planted it with white flowers, especially camellias – Madame Chanel's signature flower – and we won a Gold. The press and TV coverage was incredible: everybody was interested, worldwide – not just in Britain. This was a way to have everyone talk about Chanel and to enhance the brand of the House of Chanel." Despite this, there are no plans for another Chanel garden – after a major victory there is no point in revisiting the battlefield.

The glossy magazines *Harpers & Queen* and *Country Life* have both sponsored gardens. *Country Life's* was a one-off, designed by Rupert Golby to celebrate its centenary in 1997. "We had a show garden because gardening is central to the magazine. In a hundred years we had never sponsored a garden at Chelsea,

"A Cottage Garden at Railway Cuttings" was designed by the Julian Dowle Partnership for the Sunday Express in 1994. It conjured up all those colourful plots of land that flash past passengers during a train journey.

£50,000 from the sponsors, Hiscox Insurance, and a similar amount from *Country Life*'s publishers, IPC. "It was a great deal of money for us and IPC were very generous, yet we still had to beg, borrow, and steal for the garden," Aslet added. An unexpected benefit was that both he and the magazine felt much closer to the gardening world and the RHS as a result. Nonetheless, like Chanel, *Country Life* is not planning another garden yet: perhaps it will have to wait for the bicentenary in 2097.

Harpers & Queen have had a longer commitment to Chelsea, with gardens in 1994, 1996, and 1998, all co-sponsored by Cartier. Their 1998 design was based on Prince Charles's garden at Highgrove. "It was very, very successful," according to *Harpers & Queen* Managing Editor, Shirley Freeman. Our readers "always look out for our garden at Chelsea, because they have learnt about it in advance in the magazine," said *Harpers & Queen*'s Editor, Fiona Macpherson. "It becomes both a meeting place and a discussion point (we usually win a major prize). Our editorial staff enjoy manning the stand during the Chelsea week, but they're not strong on which rose is 'Rambling Rector' and which 'Kiftsgate', even though they know their Gucci from their Prada." Thus, for a change, the readers can preach to the writers. It is not only the show garden that creates a sense of kudos but also access to the Gala Preview. "Tickets are like gold dust. The RHS always restricts the number

MAGAZINE MONEY

Financed by Country Living, this "Decorative Kitchen Garden" won a Gold Medal for its designer Rupert Golby in 1995. The striking white bench nestled among climbing roses, ornamental onions, irises, peonies, and catmint.

and we felt it was appropriate for our centenary," said the magazine's Editor, Clive Aslet. "It worked incredibly well. Golby's garden was brilliant and in the spirit of *Country Life*. The magazine is concerned with architecture, gardens, wildlife, the countryside, the environment, and the fine and decorative arts — and all these subjects could be found in our garden and so reinforced our centenary in people's minds. We gained a Gold and our garden was also very popular — we were mobbed." The garden cost about £100,000 — one of the most expensive ever — with

CLEMATIS SIEBOLDII VAR. ALBA
(now known as Clematis florida 'Sieboldii')
Award of Merit 1921
Exhibited by Ellen Willmott

of tickets, because there is no point to the Preview if it is packed," added Freeman.

The *Daily Express* sponsored show gardens for more than 30 years but for different reasons to *Harpers & Queen* – the *Express* uses the gardens to publicize its chosen charities. In 1999 the *Express* was campaigning for children's charities, so the ex-Barnardo's boy and top fashion designer, Bruce Oldfield, collaborated with their garden designer, James Alexander-Sinclair. The resulting "Horti-Couture" garden combined not only haute couture and garden design but also adults and children. "We got a fabulous response," said their Press Officer, Kate Hammond.

Christie's Fine Art Auctioneers are relatively new sponsors, having backed George Carter's "Birds' Buffet" (his 1998 design for Flora for Fauna) and in 1999 supported his "Sculpture in the Garden", which won a Gold Medal. Their European Marketing Director Paul Hewitt believed that "Chelsea has a unique and fashionable role and attracts wealthy people who want to spend their money on art.

Christie's is seen as a very traditional, conservative company, but we felt we could use a traditional venue to make a contemporary statement. Our concept was to give classic inspiration modern treatment. We wanted to be seen as forward-looking, influencing contemporary art in our own way. We invited key clients who were interested in gardens to our Gala Preview party, which was hosted by our Chairman of Christie's Europe, Christopher Balfour."

Dee Nolan, former Editor of *You* magazine of the *Mail on Sunday*, considered Chelsea to be both a glamorous venue and a barometer of fashion. "In good years it's an opportunity to see the very best garden design in Britain – an unbeatable resource of ideas and inspiration. We hope that all our gardens have had a resonance that strikes a chord in the lives of our readers, even though only a tiny percentage of them are actually going to see the garden at Chelsea. We championed the cause of organic food production and gardening in 1999, for example, and we had an amazing response from readers – especially the younger, urban ones."

You caters especially for women readers and Nolan had noticed that gardening has become an increasingly feminine interest. "It is not a superficial interest but a manifestation of a genuine need. One of the jobs of an editor is to see in which direction the readers are moving – and to join them at the right time."

Nolan's very first Chelsea garden was in 1991, for the now-defunct magazine *Metropolitan Home*. Dan Pearson was its relatively untried designer, and its inspiration was an urban enclosure based on a medieval garden. When the magazine closed, Yardley stepped in as sponsor. "It won a Gold Medal – and when I saw it I really wept that it wasn't mine any more," sighed Nolan. That's Chelsea for you.

REGULAR SPONSORS
Many show gardens are backed by newspapers such as the Mail on Sunday's You *magazine, which financed "Sally Clarke's Kitchen Garden" (above) in 1996 and the organic kitchen garden surrounding Marston & Langinger's conservatory (left) in 1999. Both these exhibits were designed by Stephen Woodhams.*

THE MEDIA

GREEDY GOAT

Charlie Dimmock and the goat mascot of the Welsh Guards helped promote the Greenfingers Appeal during the 1999 Press Day. The goat gained particular attention when it ate a rose.

AS ONE OF THE MOST important horticultural events in the world, Chelsea has immense prestige. If you win a medal here, you have won the gardening Olympics, although – unlike a traditional event at the Olympics – any number of exhibitors may be awarded a Gold Medal. If you exhibit at Chelsea, you are likely to boast about it for many years hence. To impress important clients or horticultural gurus, you invite them to the Gala Preview. If you want to introduce an important new plant, a pioneering lawn mower, or a charity designed to save an endangered duck, the Chelsea Flower Show is where you do it, particularly on Press Day, which is the Monday before the show officially opens. This is the day for the press to see and be seen, even though the RHS has now invited the press in for the previous two days.

On Press Day exhibitors invite a most extraordinary list of celebrities, cherubic children, animals (banned for the rest of the week), and steel bands in the hope that they will catch the eyes of the assembled 1,000 international media folk, ranging from journalists on the glossy gardening magazines to Japanese TV reporters. The guest list provided by the RHS Press Office for Monday, 24 May 1999 revealed the fascinating range of eye-catchers who turned up for that Press Day. Jane Asher (the cake-maker and actress) was there to celebrate the 40th anniversary of the National Association of Flower Arrangement Societies (NAFAS) and the launch of their special sweet pea 'Ruby Anniversary'. Raymond Blanc (of the Manoir aux Quat' Saisons restaurant) had come to draw attention to Newington Nurseries' conservatory plants; directly below him on the Press Office guest list were two lifeboatmen in uniform, celebrating 175 years of saving lives at sea and sponsored by Gateshead Metropolitan Borough Council. Flora for Fauna, which lobbies for conservation, had brought in an eclectic mixture of personalities – Anita Brookner (novelist), Rolf Harris (entertainer), Sir Roy Strong (garden writer and former director of the Victoria & Albert Museum), and four Chelsea pensioners – to point out secret places in ordinary gardens where small creatures can survive. Nigella Lawson ('domestic goddess') was at Marston & Langinger's conservatory stand cooking meals from organic vegetables, and the Chairman of Worcestershire County Council and "other dignatories" were launching the new county rose, 'Worcestershire', which is the 18th in Mattocks's money-making County Series®.

Charlie Dimmock (gardening presenter of television's *Ground Force*) made several appearances on Press Day 1999. Some Welsh Guards wheeled her about the show in a barrow as part of the National Wheelbarrow challenge to raise money for the Greenfingers Appeal on Notcutts stand.

With a Scot dressed in National Trust for Scotland tartan, Charlie Dimmock was next seen on the National Trust for Scotland's stand, where she publicized their new tartan. She also held an interview opportunity, called "In bed with Charlie", on the KinderGarden Plants stand.

Alan Titchmarsh (Charlie Dimmock's *Ground Force* co-presenter) was almost as ubiquitous. He was on the Barleywood stand to launch garden sundries, and again at the Wyevale Garden Centres show garden for the same purpose. He later appeared at Myles Challis's "Cascade Garden".

WIDE RANGE OF GUESTS

No celebrity is too abstruse to qualify, as the press office guest list for 2003 proved. The list also proves how willing all lesser celebrities are to strut their stuff in front of wall to wall TV cameras. Though the serious gardening press will have no truck with half-dressed models lounging on beds of pansies, the nationals just love a sexy picture, which, of course, the exhibitors know very well. This may be why Tamara Beckwith was seen modelling a Shanghai Tang outfit for the Laurent Perrier, *Harpers & Queen* garden designed by Tom Stuart-Smith (which coincidentally, won the best garden award). We were told that Ms. Beckwith's clothes were "especially selected to complement the *Cornus kousa*", in the planting.

Other celebs listed in 2003 included a bevy of model beauties and socialites such as Jodie Kidd and the perennial Jerry Hall

along with Tara Palmer-Tomkinson and Ivana Trump. Liz Hurley, definitely A list, didn't show. But there are still strong links between the chic of Chelsea and the chic of the fashion houses with such designers as John Rocha, Bruce Oldfield (who has helped design a garden), Julien MacDonald and Nicole Farhi among Chelsea visitors.

Actors and actresses are always willing to appear and, in 2003 we had Nigel Havers, Maureen Lipman, Helen Mirren (about to star nude in *Calendar Girls*) and ex-*Good Life* 's

ATTRACTING PUBLICITY
Desmond Lynam appeared at The Scotts Co. stand in 1999, where he introduced a Dianthus named after himself, and also, with Jimmy Hill, Desmond Wilcox, and Esther Rantzen, at the launch of "A New Beginning", for Marie Curie Cancer Research.

WHOLESOME FOOD EXPERT
Nigella Lawson made a guest appearance in 1999 in the organic herb and vegetable garden designed by Stephen Woodhams and sponsored by You magazine.

VIRTUOSA VIOLINIST

Musicians in groups and individually often help to promote exhibitors' stands at Chelsea. Here celebrity violinist Vanesssa Mae appears on David Steven's 1997 garden, "A Creative Century", which celebrated the centenary of its sponsor, EMI.

WRONG FLOWERS

Leslie Ash and Rory Bremner are carefully posed by photographers smelling two eye-catching flowers, which were, however, ornamental onions (Allium) and not sweet-scented at all.

Penelope Keith. Cooks too, seem to like looking at flowers, with Raymond Blanc, a perfectionist when it comes to vegetable varieties in his Manoir aux Quat' Saisons, Phil Vickery and Nigel Slater who is increasingly working with gardens, encouraged by co-*Observer* writer, Monty Don. And then there were the faces of Anthea Turner, Carol Vorderman, Anneka Rice and Esther Rantzen, who don't have a great deal in common other than celebrity status.

Clearly not on any press office celeb list however, are the great gardeners such as Christopher Lloyd (who has never shown anything at Chelsea) and designers like Bunny Guinness, Sir Terence Conran and George Carter. They are there not only for

inspiration, but also to see what not to do.

All the razzmatazz is swept away for the Monday afternoon, when the Royal Family visits Chelsea in the sort of relaxed and uncrowded conditions of which you and I can only dream. During this visit, only accredited photographers among the media are allowed to remain at the show. On Peter J. Smith's stand, history was being made in 1999. For the first time ever, the Queen, in her role as Sovereign Head of the Order of St John, officially launched a plant –

DIFFERENT HAZARDS ▷

Television teams from all over the world turn up to record the famous faces at Chelsea. While cranes and forklift trucks were the danger during the run-up to the show, on Press Day cables, tripods, and cameras have to be avoided.

Alstroemeria 'Crusader Lily' to celebrate the Order's 900th anniversary. Also present were Lady Barttelot (Chief President of St John Ambulance) and Nic Donovan (Facilities Manager at St John Ambulance) dressed as an 11th-century crusader knight. For the plant's first three years on sale, Peter J. Smith of Chanctonbury Nurseries donated £1 to the Order of St John for every plant sold of *Alstroemeria* 'Crusader Lily'.

THE PLACE TO BE SEEN

Once the royal visitors have left the show, it's the moment the heavy-hitting financial firms such as 2003 Gala Preview sponsors Merrill Lynch entertain their very private clients. This is the time to see and be seen as the butterfly celebs give way to the real movers and shakers, from top politicians to the eminences grises of finance. Indeed it's not too fanciful to imagine that, among the flowers, quango chairmen and 'Tony's cronies' are selected for office. In lighter vein, it was almost certainly at the Gala Preview that the famous snap of Cherie Blair was taken with her pixie-booted guru, Carole Caplin. The *Evening Standard* reported on some of those present at a recent preview. "Where else would one see Sir John Kemp-Welch [Chairman of the Stock Exchange] and Charlie Dimmock [gardening presenter]? Or find, among the ponds, moats, and waterfalls that are the leitmotif of this year's show, the hybrid assortment of Catrina Skepper [model], Sir David Barnes [Chief Executive of AstraZeneca], the

Canadian entrepreneur Galen Weston and his wife Hilary [Lieutenant-Governor of Ontario], the Hong Kong entrepreneur David Tang, Rudolph Agnew [Chairman of the Lasmo oil company], and Santa Sebag-Montefiore [née Palmer-Tomkinson]? This is the power garden party of the year."

Victoria Mather (journalist) spotted Michael Szell (interior designer), who claimed to "have been coming to this show for 25 years. The emphasis has completely shifted from indoors, with all those begonias, to outside, to the set-piece gardens and teak furniture, because people are now using their gardens as extra rooms." Lord Astor of Hever (Conservative Party Whip), she reported, was slightly wistful. "It's so depressing coming here because it

makes one feel one's own garden is so awful."

Panama-hatted Sir Terence Conran (designer/entrepreneur), whose "Chef's Roof Garden" recently had one of the largest sites, was giving nonchalant interviews in the press tent. "Food and gardening seem to be today's rock'n'roll," he said, waving a languid hand. On Gala Preview evening he was surrounded by a milling crowd of rain-drenched bankers eager for his asparagus tips in filo pastry. "Conran's kitchen was, at one moment, crammed like an old Marx Brothers' movie," reported Victoria Mather, "with 40 heaving bodies escaping the rain and passing on the great man's exquisite, on-site-cooked canapés over each other's heads, whenever the plate made it past portly Nicholas Soames [Tory politician]."

She was greatly impressed at the high quality of celebrities at the Gala Preview. "This party is far more about sweet talking than sweet peas. When rain drove the crowd inside the Great Marquee, there was Lord Levy [who had raised £25 million for the Labour Party] by the fuchsias, as were City titans George Magan and Anthony Salz [of Freshfields]," commented Victoria Mather. While the Conservative Party was also represented at this annual extravaganza by Michael Heseltine and Peter Lilley.

MAN OF MANY SKILLS

Sir Terence Conran reflected the zeitgeist of 1999, when he combined vegetables, fruit, and flowers in his "Chef's Roof Garden" for the Evening Standard and Laurent Perrier. Here he entertains visitors, many of whom enjoyed his complimentary snacks which were served at the Gala Preview.

THE CLOTHES

THE RHS FLOWER SHOW at Chelsea is never likely to be a great fashion event. Its visitors are too much at the mercy of weather that is often changeable and extreme, to wear exotic clothing. Over the years Chelsea visitors have groaned under blinding sun in an overcrowded showground packed with reflective white canvas and melting ice-creams; they have coped with winds capable of demolishing rather than simply blowing off a smart hat; they have

MILLINERY
CONFECTION
Lady Abbott Anderson's magnificent feathered hat for Chelsea was not considered unusual among London society in 1914. Then, as now, the show was the first event of the London Season.

been very thoroughly chilled at temperatures not far above freezing; and they have been bombarded by hailstones, lightning, and almost tropical downpours. Sometimes they have endured several of these conditions within a single hour.

Gala Previews are generally typical of this variable weather and the problems of knowing what clothes to wear. They might begin in bright sunshine with bankers and their smart wives in elegantly flowing frocks strolling among the show gardens; and end in a short, sharp downpour with the same bankers and their wives drenched but undaunted. Such was the fate of the clothing at this the glitziest event in the whole Chelsea Flower Show.

HIGH HEADED
The conservatory firm Marston & Langinger found a novel way to publicize their products, but then hats at Chelsea have always ranged from the ordinary to the utterly bizarre.

Most visitors to the show arrive well-prepared: with umbrellas that can be used as parasols, and strong, comfortable shoes. Exhibitors, during the build-up to Chelsea, generally dress as gardeners do – in jeans, dungarees, T-shirts, sweaters, and stout shoes. Only when the show is about to open do they change into their best clothes.

Since the Chelsea Flower Show began in 1913, it is fascinating to observe how clothes have changed. An early photograph shows a group of men: some are wearing straw boaters flat across their heads; others are in bowlers with upturned brims, while yet another wears what looks like a billycock hat – a truncated hat with a brim like a rain gutter. What all these men have in common is watches on fob chains. Louis Cartier had designed the wristwatch ("a watch on a leather strap") for his friend the Brazilian aviator Alberto Santos Dumond in 1904. For gardeners such an invention was a much more practical workpiece than a watch on a chain, yet many Chelsea visitors and RHS officials continued to carry a fob chain, often as a status symbol. All the men in the picture are also wearing heavy, three-piece suits but that was de rigueur whether the temperature was near freezing or very hot.

FEMALE ATTIRE

The crowds at the early shows were formally dressed, with the ladies wearing afternoon or tea gowns. In the 1920s, skirts were shortened from ankle to knee length, and hats lost their tiers of flowers and feathers to become simple cloches. Many Chelsea crowd scenes of that period show almost every female visitor wearing a cloche hat; every man also has a hat – a bowler, homburg, boater, or wide-brimmed trilby.

One fashionable American was photographed in the 1930s sporting a straw hat perched at a chic 45 degree angle, a corsage on her sleek dress, a little circular handbag clutched in gloved hands, and an entire fox's pelt – from beady-eyed head to drooping tail – draped around her shoulders. Its sharp claws had not even been removed.
The day looks warm.

CHELSEA FASHIONS

These two women in the 1920s, cloche hats pulled down over their foreheads, and breasts bandaged flat, are wearing dresses that had waistlines lowered to the hips. Stunningly ill at ease, they are shaking hands through the artificially heart-shaped trunk of a topiary bay tree – a shape that was very fashionable at the time.

Perhaps she was a little extreme: the general dress code of the period was a large hat, a clutch bag, and a bias-cut floral print dress.

Floral dresses, in fact, have always been viewed as ideal Chelsea clothing, since bustles gave way to short skirts. They are constant through the glamorous 1930s as well as through the deprived late 1940s and 1950s. Even in the swinging 1960s and psychedelic 1970s, female visitors to Chelsea avoided wearing garish clothes. The 1960s, however, did see a decline in hats worn by either sex, as clothing generally became more relaxed.

TWO OF A KIND
Pauline Featherstone pauses by a double begonia that matches the decoration on her hat, while viewing exhibits in the Great Marquee during Press Day in 1964.

The move to informality has been even more striking in clothes worn by gardeners in the 20th century. Back in the 1920s, female gardeners had looked like Vita Sackville-West, with their smart lace-up shoes, gaiters or knee socks, and an adult gym slip. The hair was generally cropped fashionably. Male gardeners who were not gentry wore three-piece suits in a heavy cloth, white shirts, and

HIGH FASHION
Unusual garden clothes were worn when fashion designer Bruce Oldfield joined a model to promote the Express's fusion of gardening and fashion. He had collaborated with James Alexander-Sinclair on this "Horti-Couture" garden of 1999.

very large woollen caps placed flat on their heads. When at work they removed their jackets but not their waistcoats, and rolled up their shirt sleeves, but kept on their caps. By the 1930s trilbies seem to have replaced these caps and, after the Second World War, gardeners' outfits had a distinct look of old uniform trousers for a while.

INFORMALITY GAINS A HOLD

The great change in gardeners' clothes arrived with the general acceptance of jeans in the 1960s. Since then nothing has challenged the virtues of these strong denim trousers with rivets – even if the colour, shape, and length may slowly change with fashion. Gardeners of 50 years or more ago might well be stunned to see the modern workforce at Chelsea, who are often fit, bronzed, and muscular. Their hair may be tied back in ponytails or under bandannas, the top half of their bodies may be bare, their "trousers" are shorts, and their shoes nailed and heavy. Garden designers, working on their sites at the Royal Hospital showground, are distinguished by their unstructured pale linen suits, exotic hats from the Outback or Oregon, and mobile phones.

Apart from the ultra smart Princess Marina, Duchess of Kent in the 1930s, the Royal Family seems a little less fashion-conscious and are generally well-prepared for rainstorms. The Queen Mother favoured, in particular, feathered hats with uptilted brims and coats trimmed with yet more feathers, while the Queen prefers a neat coat, suit, or floral frock for her annual visit to the Chelsea Flower Show.

Even men's hats were declining in the 1990s – unless strong sun threatened balding heads. At the Gala Preview in 1999 only one man was wearing one and that was the Chinese multi-millionaire David Tang. "It takes a foreigner to show the English how to dress," he commented. He was also sporting an electric-blue coat. The chief female fashion accessory has over the last few years been the ubiquitous pashmina shawl, perhaps about to pass into the great antique wardrobe of history, although the pashmina has one major advantage for show visitors – its adaptability is just right for Chelsea's unpredictable weather.

FORMAL FROCK

Even bridal gowns are sometimes worn at the Chelsea Flower Show. The model Jerry Hall made a guest appearance, complete with formal bouquet and flowers strewn in her hair, at the National Trust stand in the early 1990s.

THE ROWS

THE CHELSEA FLOWER SHOW always seems to have attracted controversy; indeed some people suggest that no show would be complete without a good row. Even before the Great Spring Flower Show moved to Chelsea, in 1913, the RHS Council, on 14 May that year, was discussing the scandal of missing exhibition vases at previous shows. Over the preceding eight years the Society had lent vases to exhibitors at their Inner Temple shows, yet thousands had not been returned, and had possibly even been "purloined". The RHS felt sufficiently aggrieved to appoint an official vasekeeper, a Mr Bissit, who was to distribute the vases at the 1913 Chelsea Flower Show and, no doubt, count them back. He was to be paid £5 for this task. If

CROWD CONTROL

The one-way system introduced in the 1970s to relieve congestion in the Great Marquee was unpopular with many visitors and exhibitors.

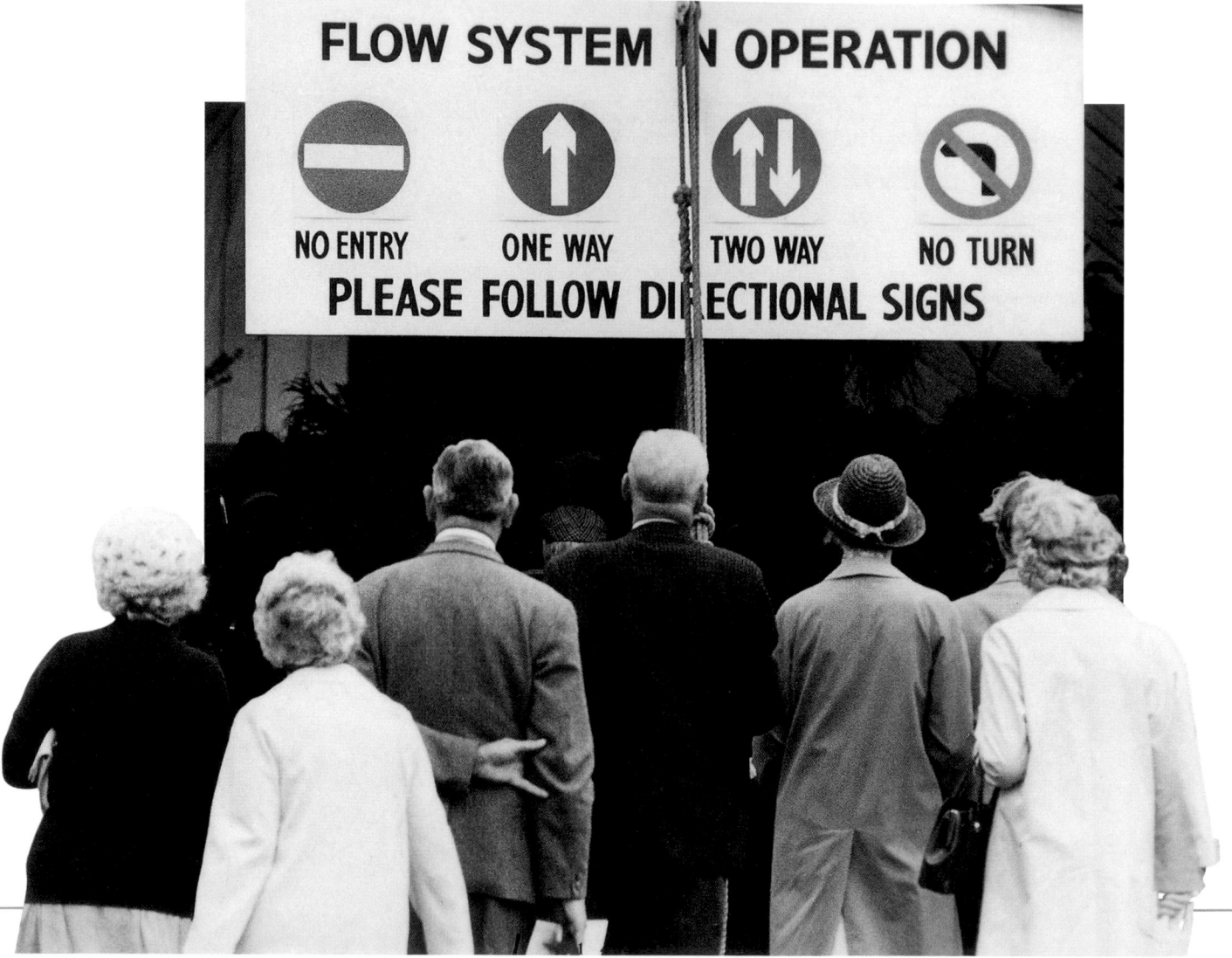

it had not been recorded in the RHS Council Minutes, this minor incident might well have vanished into oblivion – as have so many modern, equally trivial problems.

A major row in more recent times (the 1970s) was triggered by the society's attempts to regulate the Chelsea crowds, when it introduced a controversial one-way system in the Great Marquee. While this stopped visitors' ability to dart from one stand to the next, it also prevented the legendary gridlock in such a confined area. Visitors hated this restriction, because they wanted to flit about as the mood took them; they very often ignored it – and it was hard to police. Yet the controls did have the desired effect. The disappearance of the Great Marquee, however, saw the last of the comprehensive one-way system, although it still operates around the very busy outer sections of the new structure.

The show gardens had meanwhile become so popular that, at peak times, temporary one-way systems were also introduced in the early 1990s in the open, with security men holding up no-entry signs to manage visitors' wanderings.

ENTRANCE CHARGES

An even greater furore was created in 1987, when the Council decided to introduce more general crowd-control measures, by restricting ticket numbers for the 1988 show and making RHS members pay for their visit to Chelsea. Newly appointed and nervous of the safety of the 247,000 visitors to the 1987 show, Shows Director Stephen Bennett readily supported this move to limit the numbers of visitors. Some 10,000 members subsequently resigned in disgust at the Council's new policy, yet – like many

changes that are initially unpopular – it did, on balance, solve the problem.

Other controversial rules have had slightly less impact. There is, for example, a ban on garden gnomes at Chelsea. In 1993 a gnome staged a demonstration outside the show's main gates, reported *The Times*. Lampy, aged 130, and his protest caused so much trouble, because the crowds that he attracted blocked the showground entrance, that he was finally allowed into the show. The following year (1994) Lampy protested at the gnome discrimination policy by refusing to go to Chelsea and, with owner Michael Minhall, set up his own show – The Ideal Gnome Exhibition – at Nottingham.

CONTROVERSIAL COST
Some RHS members resigned in protest when the Society first started charging them for tickets to visit the Chelsea Flower Show. Until 1988, members had enjoyed free access to this event.

ROSA GLAMIS CASTLE ('**Auslevel**')
Award of Merit 1992
Exhibited by David Austin Roses.

POPULAR
MISCONCEPTION
*In 1994 there was a public
outcry when it became more
generally known that some
exhibitors did not
themselves grow all the
plants on their Chelsea
stands. Some bought them
from New Covent Garden
Market, shown here, while
others used different sources
such as specialist nurseries.*

That same year – 1994 – was a vintage one for arguments. There were protests from some exhibitors when a number of Gold Medal winners admitted that they had not grown all the plants on their stands; some had purchased their plants or flowers ready-grown from other nurseries, New Covent Garden wholesale market, or other assorted plantsellers. Joe Ambridge reported that his entire stand had been sponsored by another grower, who had cultivated the plants for him; and John Amand imported his tulip and crocus bulbs from the Netherlands. A carnation grower, Harry Armitage, had bought in one variety, 'Seville', because he hadn't enough of his own. "I come here to sell young plants, not these exhibits, and my display is really just an advert, so I don't see the harm," he told the *Daily Telegraph*.

Carol Fair of Valley Clematis Nursery showed three varieties she had not grown herself, because she wanted to help growers without stands at the show to promote their plants. "People tend to use us as a showcase. What does peeve me is when you see lots of plants from the Netherlands being unloaded on to a stand, still in their Dutch wrapping."

A *Daily Telegraph* report also revealed that many flowers for the Chelsea Flower Show came from the Zuid-Holland glasdistrict, an area of 49,000 acres (19,830 hectares) of greenhouses between Rotterdam, Gouda, and the North Sea, and that they were imported by firms such as J. van den Bos, which cultivates 1.5 million flowers a year.

Charlie Gardener, a flower merchant at New Covent Garden, claimed that Chelsea prizewinners had been buying flowers from him for decades. "You may think they are grown by the person displaying them but it is common sense that this cannot be so." Nonetheless he felt it would be a pity if bought-in flowers were banned from the show. "It would not be such a spectacle. The judges don't consider the source of the plants when awarding marks." A Dutch nurseryman added that, on the stand, credit should be given to the real grower, otherwise it was cheating.

Bennett explained the Society's policy in a letter to *The Times* in 1994. "Some firms contract out the growing of young plants; some borrow trees or shrubs from neighbouring exhibitors to complete the presentation of their displays – and this is accepted as reasonable practice and good showmanship. The Royal Horticultural Society accepts that it is generally not an attempt to deceive the public and we cannot outlaw a practice that cannot effectively be policed." Anyway, he added, what did "grown by" mean? Did the plants have to come from seeds or cuttings, did they have to be in the care of the exhibitor for a whole season, several years, or what? How can you expect a bonsai exhibitor to have grown trees older than himself? Many of Chelsea's exhibitors are clearly not growers: think of the charities, newspapers, magazines, florists, and flower arrangers, for example. Accepting that the public's interest lay primarily in the nursery trade, the RHS concluded that these exhibitors should be encouraged – but not obliged – to declare the extent to which they had – or had not – grown the plants.

This particular controversy is still unresolved. Those who grow everything themselves inevitably feel aggrieved when others are awarded medals for displays that include bought-in plants. But what of exhibitors who want to show off their own home-grown speciality in front of purchased background foliage? And should visitors be banned from enjoying spectacular new blooms just because those exhibiting at Chelsea have not grown them?

UNACCEPTABLE BEHAVIOUR

Another row in 1994 was triggered by an *Evening Standard* report revealing that part of a show garden at Chelsea had been banned. "Genteel outrage pervaded the upper echelons of the Royal Horticultural Society today after it was forced to censor one of its exhibition gardens, to protect the modesty of the public," announced the *Evening Standard*. The immodest garden, which was entitled "A Constructivist Garden", was the creation of garden designer Paul Cooper, who decided – conveniently at the last minute – that his plot was going to "accommodate human sexual needs". His garden contained white rubber sheeting for paths, black grass (*Ophiopogon planiscapus* 'Nigrescens'), a decoy wooden

fish, old herbal teabags, and a wind machine, which, if you stood on it, re-created what Cooper called "Marilyn Monroe's uplifting experience". Pictures of embracing men, hung from an *Acer negundo* tree, were promptly removed by the RHS but the teabags and wooden fish were allowed to remain.

"While appreciating that gardening is Britain's second most popular active pastime," Bennett told the *Evening Standard*, "it came as a surprise to learn that Mr Cooper intended to include the most popular pastime in his exhibit." In his letter to *The Times* Bennett explained, "Mr Cooper's original application proposed an inter-war-style domestic garden reflecting the lifestyle

COOPER'S CREATION

In 1994 Paul Cooper's "Constructivist Garden" caused a furore, because of its overtly sexual trappings. All was forgiven by 1999, however, when the designer showed "A Floating Garden" (above), which boasted buoyant containers that rested on the water like coracles.

of that era. His brief, recently submitted as the basis of the Chelsea judges' analysis, gives no indication that bedroom furniture, air blowers, or sexual activity are to be included in the design. Had there been any hint of these elements being incorporated in the garden, the Royal Horticultural Society would have taken a dim view and would have invited Mr Cooper to revise his plans."

All had been forgiven by 1999, when Paul Cooper won a Bronze Flora Medal for his "Floating Garden". He had created an attractive design of galvanized-iron containers drifting on water, and their random movements were most pleasant to watch – even if weeding was difficult.

The RHS show organizers had been similarly outraged in the 1950s. One of the many stories handed down through RHS circles is an anecdotal incident of an attempt to outlaw the activities of a flamboyant exhibitor who was displaying a rock garden. On Press Day, to attract attention to his work, he hired some lightly clad models to pose on his rocks. Such publicity-seeking is hardly novel at events such as The London Motor Show, yet Mr A. Simmonds, the RHS Secretary, was adamant that the girls had to be removed. He cited paragraph 30 of an exhibitors' schedule, which listed banned articles: those items that "may not be exhibited or used in any part of the show" included livestock "of any kind (except with special permission of the Secretary)". The Secretary did not permit and the girls were

◁ ANGRY DISSENT
The decision in 1999 to give the Best Garden Award to "The Daily Telegraph Reflective Garden" was greeted with some cries of "Foul play", especially when it was revealed that the garden was to be re-created at RHS Garden Wisley.

hurried off. The rule had been made after yet another fracas a year earlier, when a group of goats had been part of a display garden.

RECENT CONTROVERSIES
Judges and judging standards at Chelsea were criticized nationally in 1999 after "The *Daily Telegraph* Reflective Garden" won the Best Garden Award. In its gossip column *The Times* revealed that the *Telegraph* garden was destined to be a star attraction at the RHS

MIXED MATERIALS
Michael Balston's modernist design for his 1999 "The Daily Telegraph *Reflective Garden" included glass candleholders on steel spikes underplanted with* Artemisia ludoviciana *'Valerie Finnis' and* Allium cristophii.

ALLEGED PLAGIARISM

After Arabella Lennox-Boyd had been awarded a Gold Medal in 1998 for her "Contemporary Water Garden", a Belgian designer claimed that she had in fact copied one of his own gardens.

Garden Wisley, in Surrey. "Gardening experts fear that the judges' decision sits oddly with the Society's rules, which forbid it from awarding a prize to one of its own." Garden designers, some unnamed, called the link between the award and the garden's planned move to Wisley as "useful", "a hot potato", and "a scandal", and the garden's designer, Michael Balston, further fuelled the controversy when he explained, "I would not have designed the garden if it had no future." The main controversy in 1999 concerned

genetically modified crops, the increasing use of which was causing international disquiet at the time. On 25 May, Professor Philip Stott, Professor of Biogeography at the University of London, wrote in *The Times*, "What a nonsensical brouhaha over GM crops – and precisely as your horticultural correspondent glories in the Chelsea Flower Show, our annual celebration of genetic modification and biotechnology." The environmental campaigner Jill, Duchess of Hamilton agreed that plants were a celebration of genetic modification, yet felt that unease about the effects of GM crops on nature was far from a confused protest. Upset by the extravagantly hybridized blooms at Chelsea, she has started campaigning for indigenous flowers, of which there are "around 1,700 flowering species native to the British Isles," she explained.

Having previously exhibited an "Australian Garden" and "The Birds' Buffet", through the conservation charity Flora for Fauna, Jill, Duchess of Hamilton was now all the more determined to encourage awareness of British wild flowers and the food chain at future shows. "It would be such a help to the global environment if all gardening charities, especially the RHS, had policies that make conservation a priority. Although there is an outcry against the threat to wildlife from genetically modified plants, rarely has anyone publicly condemned the decline of essential food for insects – especially bees and butterflies – caused by the insatiable appetite for bigger and more spectacular blooms. Few people realize that many modified plants have often lost their nectar."

Her proposed Flora for Fauna Medal would actively encourage gardeners to combine conservation and horticulture. It would lobby for all public planting to include at least one-third of native plants; garden charities would be persuaded to broaden their scope to make Britain's native plant heritage a top priority; and nurserymen and gardeners would be asked to reduce use of polytunnels and greenhouses, thus lowering fuel and light pollution. Through such garden shows as Chelsea, Jill, Duchess of Hamilton felt it was important that the public should learn to

appreciate the use of real plants in real seasons and to stop relying on giant flowers forced to bloom at artificial times.

Such conservation issues are certain to be in the forefront of controversial issues for years to come, because the Chelsea Flower Show is both an arbiter of garden taste and a barometer of future concerns.

ENVIRONMENTAL CONCERNS
Jill, Duchess of Hamilton campaigned in 1999 for greater use of native British plants at shows such as Chelsea, at the expense of genetically modified ones. Here she poses in front of her and Jon Bannenberg's "Australian Garden" of 1994.

THE FINALE

BEFORE I EVER BECAME interested in the Chelsea Flower Show – or even knew when it happened – I arrived at Victoria Station one Friday afternoon in late May to find it utterly transformed. It looked as though Great Birnam Wood (from Shakespeare's *Macbeth*) had reached the terminus. Elderly gents in Panamas, sweating and red-faced, struggled with massive palms in black plastic pots, which they clutched against their blue blazers. Sensible county ladies in stout shoes sprouted ferns from the pockets of their good-quality tweed suits and hostas from their wheeled shopping baskets, while middle-aged couples, dragging bundles of unseasonally flowering pelargoniums, shouted encouragement to each other as they ran at full pelt to reach a train. The London commuters treated all this pandemonium as part of their normal day; it takes more than a horticultural explosion to excite these work-weary travellers. For the newly arrived foreigners, who had only recently flown into Gatwick for a city-break in London, it was all rather startling. Was England always like this?

△ FINAL FEELINGS

Visitors and exhibitors view the break-up of the show with mixed emotions. It is sad to witness the whole illusion being destroyed, but it is also a unique chance to buy exhibition-quality and often unusual plants.

▽ HOPEFUL CUSTOMERS

As break-up of the show approaches, visitors start assembling by the stands on which they have ordered plants. Although exhibitors are not allowed to sell anything before a bell rings, Notcutts (here) can at least distribute bags for future purchases.

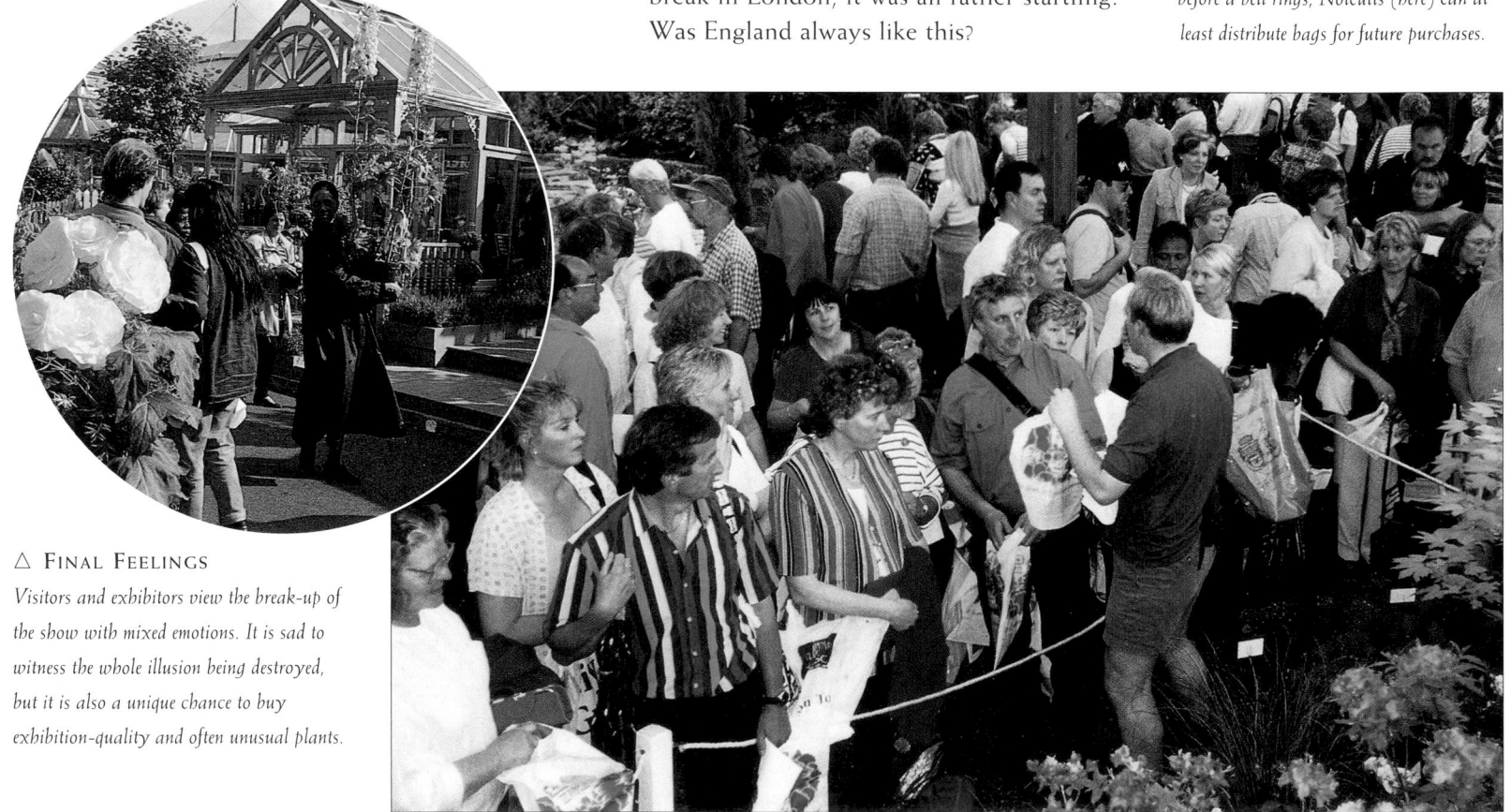

REMOVAL MEN

As visitors carry off their booty (right), the plants that did not sell or the cut flowers that died during the show are quickly bundled up and removed by contractors (left) or the exhibitors themselves.

The answer is, of course, yes it is always like this on just one day a year: on "Break-up Day", when the Chelsea Flower Show closes. The events on this day are part of the Chelsea tradition, even if, like the show itself, the rules sometimes change. At a preordained time on the Friday afternoon, the plants on the exhibitors' stands in the Pavilion may be removed from the displays and sold to Chelsea visitors. This annual rummage sale used to start at 5pm, half an hour before the whole show officially closed. In 1999, bowing to pressure from frantic public and exhausted exhibitors to allow a little more time for the great break-up, the RHS decreed that the plant sale could start at 4.30pm, allowing a whole hour in which the glory of the Chelsea Flower Show is split, plundered, and dragged away on buses, bikes, taxis, and Tubes by delighted visitors.

During the final two hours of the show, gradually and surreptitiously people erect their wheeled shopping baskets; others, as if from nowhere, appear with large wheelbarrows; porters' trolleys are brought through the show gates with stout cartons attached. People who have secreted black plastic bin liners around their waists – despite the sometimes tropical conditions at the show – quietly remove them, while those in wheelchairs sense their advantage. Visitors steadily start to mass around the most popular stands, and some well-prepared exhibitors hand out plastic bags.

You can hear people who have not ordered plants in advance begin to plan their strategy. They may fancy plants from stands hundreds of yards apart: some will be tiny and easily carried, while others 10ft (3m) tall with waving blooms. Buyers may have to run from one stand to another,

dragging spoils as they go. How can they purchase everything before the show gates shut at 5.30pm? Should they split up and arrange a meeting place outside the showground? Should they soldier on together (and it is like a planned invasion), dragging the unfortunate plants between them? Should one do the queuing and the other the packing? Husbands tell wives how to organize their strategy; wives advise husbands how best to carry their shopping. Some cheerful ladies together signal their joint determination to win at all costs; while teenagers are charged with guarding a cache of plants as parents forage for more.

By 4pm the crowds are expectantly thronging six deep around stands such as Fibrex, where flowering pelargoniums will soon be sold to the fortunate few. Other visitors once surrounded the Notcutts stand, where, high on the Chillianwallah Monument, the nursery staff climbed to take photographs of the scrum beneath.

An announcement over the tannoy reminds visitors that not a single plant can be sold until a bell rings. On pain of banishment from Chelsea – possibly for ever – the exhibitors hold back. Meanwhile one standholder is unsentimentally tossing away armfuls of spent, cut tulips, their petals drooping and dropping, now their job is done. No one is around this stall for they are selling nothing. Nor are they milling around Cheshire Herbs' stand, where half an hour earlier it was impossible to see the display.

◁ PRECIOUS PURCHASES

In late afternoon, on the final day of the show, hordes of visitors may be seen struggling with their shopping. They often underestimate the size and weight of these acquisitions.

Because she does not sell her plants, the owner is left alone; her display is no longer of interest to Chelsea visitors.

When the bell signalling the start of the plant sale finally rings at 4.30pm, mayhem breaks loose. Wearing a T-shirt announcing that she's "A Knackered Gardener", a young exhibitor still finds enough energy to climb the trellis on one stand so she can tear the display to pieces. Everywhere in that huge covered area the plants bred for the most important week of their lives are ripped down and sold to eager bidders.

The Chelsea Flower Show, in all its artificial perfection, is destroyed in an hour. The fountains stop playing; the streams cease to run; while the towers of carrots and cauliflowers will be supper tonight for their exhibitors. There is a compulsive urge to take part in the sell-off, possibly because these splendid plants are often sold cheaply – and who can resist a bargain? – but also, more to the point, because they are a remembrance of things past. When you tweak a scented leaf off a pelargonium in your dining room or divide a particularly subtle iris, you are reminded of that show. One plant represents Chelsea 1994 and yet another recalls Chelsea 2003 – they are living history.

By 5.30pm, another Chelsea Flower Show has become history. Hundreds of contented people pour out of the show gates, laden with plants, and head towards the taxi ranks, the astonished bus queues, the nearest Tube, or the ever-tolerant commuters at Victoria station. They've all acquired a little bit of Chelsea, a plant or 20 for their gardens – their own piece of the greatest flower show in the world. It's all been worthwhile.

CLOSE DOWN

Here someone has thoughtfully covered the face of this statue so it does not have to witness the surrounding destruction, as stands are torn down and show gardens dug up. Even statues have their pride.

SURVIVORS' GUIDE

THE BEST WAY TO GAIN FULL ENJOYMENT from Chelsea is to treat it like a military operation and plan strategy in advance. Personally I enjoy the preliminary decision-making as much as the event itself, especially if everything works out right. I start by organizing tickets to the show well in advance, then work out what clothes to wear, depending on the weather forecast the day before. I reduce the contents of my bags or pockets to the absolute minimum while adding such essential extras as notebook and pencil (ballpoints won't write in the rain), empty carrier bags for any purchases, plenty of cash (not heavy pound coins), and a list of what I want to see.

On show day I am up early to make sure I reach the grounds in good time. (If you live out of London you could stay at a hotel near the Royal Hospital to save your energy entirely for the show.) I arrive at the Chelsea gates determined to enjoy every last minute of my day, meet gardening friends, and have a delicious lunch. And I come away laden with the wheelbarrow loads of ideas that Chelsea always offers. Here are some useful hints and tips from regular Chelsea goers.

PAPER HAT

In extremis, any head protection will do, but it is better to come prepared with a folding sun or waterproof hat.

BEFORE YOU SET OFF

- Make sure you know your exact route to the Royal Hospital, especially from the nearest public transport points. The main entrance for the public is the Bull-Ring Gate on the Chelsea Embankment. The other public entrance is the London Gate, which is off Royal Hospital Road.
- Sloane Square is the nearest Underground station, ⅓ mile (½km) from the showground; just follow the crowds walking to the show.
- Victoria, the nearest mainline station, is 1 mile (1.6km) away and is quite a walk, especially at the end of the day, but there is a shuttle bus.
- The nearest bus routes are along Royal Hospital Road, Chelsea Bridge Road, and Pimlico Road. Many other buses stop around Sloane Square.
- Taxis can come right up to the Bull-Ring and London gates, beside the ground. If the roads are very congested, ask to be dropped off somewhere easy, like Sloane Square.
- Courtesy buses run to and from Battersea Park, where you may be able to park your car or motorbike – but don't bet on it.
- A show ticket will also cover the admission of a companion in the case of a wheelchair user or visually handicapped visitor.
- Temperatures can be extreme. Make sure you are prepared by wearing flexible clothing.
- It may rain torrentially during your visit to Chelsea. Umbrellas can be a menace in crowds, so consider a waterproof hat and raincoat instead.
- At other times the sun can be almost tropically hot, so take suitable sun protection, for example sunscreen and a wide-brimmed hat.

- Always wear sensible, comfortable shoes. Flat, waterproof soles are best, because the ground can become muddy if there is heavy rain.
- Arrive as early as you can at the show, so you are ahead of the main crowds.
- Babies and children under five are not admitted to Chelsea. They wouldn't enjoy the show – and nor would you.
- The only animals allowed into the grounds (apart from Press Day) are guide dogs.
- There is a left luggage area at the showground (see Services section of the official catalogue for its position), but it is best to travel light.

ON ARRIVAL AT THE SHOWGROUND

- Buy the official Chelsea Flower Show catalogue as soon as you enter the grounds, or even in advance, and read it carefully. It can save you time.
- The catalogue has a helpful list of cafés, restaurants, and champagne bars under the Services section. This gives locations, opening times, and types of meal that are offered.
- Using the map in the back cover of the catalogue, find out where facilities such as toilets and eating areas are placed.
- Recheck the show's opening times in the catalogue, so that you can make the most of your visit.

OTHER INVALUABLE ADVICE

- Never leave anything to the last minute. It can take a surprising time to weave through the crowds.
- Always plan to visit the toilet away from the lunchtime rush, when there may be long queues.
- Your ticket does not permit you to leave the show and return. If you are there for a mealtime, you will need to eat within the grounds.
- If you want to have lunch, plan that early, to avoid the main rush at the various catering outlets.
- There is a bank at the showground (see Services section of the catalogue). It will change foreign currency, too.

BULL-RING GATE

This is the main entrance to the Chelsea Flower Show. Remember, once you leave the show, your ticket will not allow you back in again.

- The Services section of the catalogue also details visitors' official meeting places, a counter for lost property, how to track down lost children, and where there are First Aid posts.
- The RHS provides a free gardening-advice service to visitors (see Services section of the catalogue).
- Exits from the showground are well-signposted within the ground and are indicated on the map on the inside front cover of the catalogue as well as described in the Services section.
- The show can be very tiring. Take it easy.
- Try to leave before the main crowds. Buses and taxis often become overwhelmed by the extra demand.
- Plants can be bought only during the sell-off at the end of the final day; but be prepared – it's like the first day of the sales, only the plants are heavier.
- If you want to buy plants, you may have to carry them for a long time, because the show becomes very congested with everyone leaving at once on the final day. Take your own heavyweight plastic sack or collapsible trolley to carry your purchases.
- And remember, you are there to enjoy yourself.

INDEX

BIBLIOGRAPHY

CLIFTON-MOGG, CAROLINE. "The Christie's Sculpture Garden" in *Christie's Magazine*, London, May 1999.

EDWARDS, COLIN. *Delphiniums: The Complete Guide*, Marlborough, Crowood Press, 1989.

FLETCHER, H.R. *The Story of the Royal Horticultural Society 1804–1968*, Oxford, Oxford University Press, 1969.

Gardeners' Chronicle 1913–1988, title then changed to *Horticultural Week* 1988–.

HADFIELD, MILES. *A History of British Gardening*, Feltham, Spring Books, rev. edn 1969.

LANGDON, BRIAN. *The Tuberous Begonia*, London, Cassell, 1969.

MCLAREN, CHRISTABEL (Aberconway, Lady Christabel). *A Wiser Woman? A Book of Memories*, London, Hutchinson, 1966.

MARSDEN-SMEDLEY, HESTER. *The Chelsea Flower Show*, London, Constable, 1976.

WHITEN, FAITH AND GEOFF. *The Chelsea Flower Show*, London, Elm Tree Books in association with the Royal Horticultural Society, 1982.

ACKNOWLEDGEMENTS

Leslie Geddes-Brown would like to thank the Royal Horticultural Society for their co-operation with this book. She is particularly grateful to the staff in the Shows Department, under Stephen Bennett, who stopped to answer no doubt infuriating queries when they were already very busy preparing for a show.

The publishers would like to thank the following for their kind permission to reproduce their photographs.
KEY: b=bottom; bc=bottom centre; bl=bottom left; br=bottom right; c=centre; cl=centre left; cr=centre right; l=left; r=right; t=top; tc=top centre; tl=top left; tr=top right
GPL=Garden Picture Library; HP=Hugh Palmer; PH=Photos Horticultural; PB=Peter Baistow; RHS=Royal Horticultural Society; SW-Steve Wooster

1 Andrew Lawson; 2 HP; 3 PH; 4 RHS, Wisley/Lindley Library; 5 RHS, Wisley; 6 Peter Beales Roses/Bob Hobbs; 8 PH; 9 GPL/Marijke Heuff; 10/11 DK Images/SW; 12 Hulton Archive/Getty Images; 13 Notcutts; 14bl Hulton Archive/Getty Images; 14tr PH; 15tl, cr Notcutts; 16bc GPL/Vaughan Fleming; 16tl RHS, Wisley/Lindley Library; 17 Blackmore and Langdon; 18 Hulton Archive/Getty Images; 19 Hulton Archive/Getty Images; 20tr RHS, Wisley/Lindley Library; 20cl Topham Picturepoint; 21 Hulton Archive/Getty Images; 22tl, br RHS, Wisley: Lindley Library; 23 Hulton Archive/Getty Images; 24tl Hulton Archive/Getty Images; 24 PH; 25tr GPL/Tim MacMillan; 25tl RHS, Wisley/Lindley Library; 26 Hulton Archive/Getty Images; 27cr Illustrated London News Picture Library; 27bl RHS, Wisley/Lindley Library; 28br Hulton Archive/Getty Images; 28cl Illustrated London News Picture Library; 28tc RHS, Wisley/Lindley Library; 29bl Hulton Archive/Getty Images; 29tr Illustrated London News Picture Library;

30tr John Glover; 30tl Pa Photos/John Stillwell; 31tl Hulton Archive/Getty Images; 31br Pa Photos/John Stillwell; 32 DK Images/SW/ "A City Space" designed by Mark Anthony Walker, Chelsea 2000; 33 Jerry Harpur; 34 GPL/Tim MacMillan; 34tl Hulton Archive/Getty Images; 35tr GPL/Alec Scaresbrook; 36tr PB; 37bl Hugh Palmer; 37cr PH; 38tl PB; 39br PB; 39tl PH; 40bl RHS, Wisley; 40cr RHS, Wisley/Dominic Turner; 41 PB; 42bc PB; 42tr PH; 43br PB; 44tr PB; 44bl Andrew Lawson; 45bl, br PH; 46 Marston & Langinger Ltd; 47br PB; 47tl PH; 48 PB; 49c Andrew Lawson; 50cl GPL/Georgia Glynn-Smith; 50tr PH; 51bl Hulton Archive/Getty Images/Reg Speller; 52bl PB; 52tr GPL/Georgia Glynn-Smith ; 53 PB; 54tl Hulton Archive/Getty Images; 55tl HP; 56tl GPL/Georgia Glynn-Smith; 56br HP; 57 GPL/Georgia Glynn-Smith; 58bl Hulton Archive/Getty Images/Reg Spellwe; 58br PH; 58t Piggotts; 59cr RHS, Wisley; 60t Hulton Archive/Getty Images; 60bl PH; 61bl Piggotts; 61tr RHS, Wisley; 62tl PB; 63b Hulton Archive/Getty Images; 64cr PH; 64l SW; 65tr PB; 65bl PH; 66br GPL/Georgia Glynn-Smith; 66tl PH; 67r HP; 68tl HP; 68bl RHS, Wisley/Lindley Library; 69tr Gardner; 69br RHS, Wisley; 70cl PB; 70bc Hulton Archive/Getty Images; 71tl PH; 71br RHS, Wisley; 72b Hulton Archive/Getty Images; 73t Hulton Archive/Getty Images; 74tr GPL/Roger Hyam; 74bl Stapeley Water Gardens; 75t GPL; Tim MacMillan; 76 Clive Nichols; 77 GPL/John Glover; 78bl GPL/SW; 78tr SW; 79 GPL/Ron Sutherland; 80c GPL/SW; 80tl Clive Nichols; 81cr Clive Nichols; 82cr GPL/Jerry Pavia; 82l SW; 83tr Hulton Archive/Getty Images; 84tl RHS, Wisley/Lindley Library; 84br Waterer's Landscape plc; 85t PB; 86 PB/ "Evolution" designed by Piet Oudo and Arne Maynard and Gardens Illustrated Magazine, Chelsea 2000; 87 DK Images/SW/Laurent-Perrier and Harpers & Queen, Tom Stuart-Smith, Chelsea 2003; 88bl PB; 88tl DK Images/SW/ "Yorkshire Forward" by Julian Dowle, Chelsea 2003; 89 SW; 90bl HP; 90t SW; 91l DK Images/SW/ "A Garden in Homage to Le Notre" by Tom Stuart-Smith, Chelsea 2000; HP; 92br GPL/John Glover; 92l SW; 93 John Glover; 94 SW; 95l, r SW; 96bl,br PB; 97tl,bl PB; 97r SW; 98 George Carter; 98bl Marianne Majerus Photography; 99c George Carter; 100tl Marianne Majerus Photography, (tr); 101 Marianne Majerus Photography; 102 Marianne Majerus Photography; 103br SW; 104 SW; 105 Marianne Majerus Photography; 106 PB; 107 PB; 108bl GPL/JS Sira; 108tr PH; 109 Blackmore and Langdon, 1985/4; 110 Blackmore and Langdon; 111tl,r Blackmore and Langdon; 112 HP; 113 PH; 118tr,bl Medwyn Williams; 119bl,r Medwyn Williams; 120tr, bl The Interior Archive/Simon McBride; 121 The Interior Archive/Simon McBride; 122tr Notcutts; 122bl PH; 123 PH; 124 Notcutts; 125tl, tr PH; 126 GPL/Ron Sutherland; 127 Clive Nichols; 128 HP; 129 Clive Nichols; 130tl GPL/Ron Sutherland; 130cr PH; 131 HP; 132 GPL/Ron Sutherland; 133cb PB; 133tr HP; 134 Notcutts; 135cl, br Rex Features; 136tl Alpha London/Richard Chambury; 136br Rex Features/Nils Jorgensen; 137 HP; 138tl Rex Features; 138br Rex Features/Nils Jorgensen; 139 SW; 140bl PB; 140tr Hulton Archive/Getty Images; 141 RHS, Wisley/Lindley Library; 142tr PB; 142bl Hulton Archive/Getty Images; 143 PB; 144 Hulton Archive/Getty Images; 145tc PB; 145br GPL/Howard Rice; 146 Robert Harding Picture Library; 147 GPL/Ron Sutherland; 148 SW; 149 SW; 150 SW; 151 HP; 152cl Jerry Harpur; 152br Notcutts; 153tl PB; 153tr RHS, Wisley; 154 HP; 155 HP; 156 Hulton Archive/Getty Images; 157 Alpha London/Dave Chancellor.

All other images © Dorling Kindersley

For further information see: www.dkimages.com